ONE INCARNATE TRUTH

ONE INCARNATE TRUTH
Christianity's Answer to Spiritual Chaos

EDITED BY UWE SIEMON-NETTO

From UPI's "Christ and Postmodernity" Series

CONCORDIA PUBLISHING HOUSE · SAINT LOUIS

These essays were previously published as part of UPI's wire service from November 2000 through May 2001.

Copyright © 2002 Concordia Publishing House
3558 S. Jefferson Avenue, St. Louis, MO 63118-3968
Manufactured in the United States of America

1 2 3 4 5 6 7 8 9 10 11 10 09 08 07 06 05 04 03 02

CONTENTS

PUBLISHER'S PREFACE

Concordia Publishing House, the publishing arm of The Lutheran Church—Missouri Synod, seeks to produce solid resources for use by Christians in the twenty-first century. We take seriously our role to develop and distribute resources that equip readers to think critically about Christian faith, life, and history.

The following essays are reprinted with permission from the United Press International series "Christ and Postmodernity." As noted in the introduction, this collection gathers insightful essays on the postmodern world from a variety of Christian clergy and laity, all of whom confess Christ and the Gospel of forgiveness, life, and salvation as the one hope for postmodern men and women. While different traditions and theological perspectives are represented here, each author demonstrates how Christianity relates to key themes and issues in contemporary philosophy, literature, the arts, and culture in general. The essays address the social, political, economic, and cultural contexts in which Christians "live and move and have our being," what Lutheran's traditionally have called God's "kingdom of the left hand." While not directly proclaiming the Gospel, together the essays point to Christ "and the truth that is in Jesus" (Ephesians 4:21), the antidote to the present-day, postmodern chaos.

Our goal is to offer this book as a dialogue on the meaning of Christian faith in the contemporary world and to assist Christians to think critically about Christ and His significance for postmodern life.

Introduction

THE TRUTH VS. "TRUTHS"

UWE SIEMON-NETTO

What is postmodernity? Before the terrorist attacks on New York and Washington D. C. on September 11, 2001, this question seemed little more than a topic for polite discourse among academics and pundits in Europe and North America. Some fine scholars, such as Gene Edward Veith, author of the first essay in this volume, defined this era beautifully and tried to warn us of its perils. But others denied postmodernity's existence and, therefore, declined to contribute to this collection of reflections, which is based on a series commissioned by United Press International before airplanes hijacked by suicidal fanatics struck the World Trade Center and the Pentagon.

Still other scholars averred that postmodernity may have been around, but it collapsed before it ever got off the ground. If the profusion of homemade and ever-changing "truths" was postmodernity's chief property, they suggested, then the world had perhaps already turned the corner. These scholars pointed to the rapid growth of the confessional and renewal movements in mainline denominations, especially the Presbyterian and the Methodist churches. And they drew comfort from the emergence of a young elite, mainly Lutheran and Reformed, that seeks to reconnect with the confessions, liturgies, and art forms of the sixteenth century, asserting that the world had gone awry in the subsequent eras, especially during the Enlightenment and the French Revolution.

Then came September 11 and its consequences. It was troubling enough that men with a clear, though mistaken, set of values managed to execute a well-coordinated attack on America's power centers, financial and military. More ominous still, from a theologian's point of view, was the popular reaction to this event. It was all very well that Americans of all political persuasions closed rank and developed patriotic fervor. European critics were supercilious in ridiculing this turn of events instead of watching with awe as Americans fused into one large family while under attack. The Old World has lost this enviable aptitude because of the perversions of patriotism in its recent past. But this volume is not about secular sentiments of this sort. It concerns itself with matters of faith, and in this area, America's post–September 11 attitudes seem disconcerting.

The day after the terrorists struck, Rabbi Stephen Weisman of Temple Solel in Bowie, Maryland, one of my favorite Jewish interlocutors, expressed hope that the nation would pay heed to this wake-up call. At first it evidently did. Americans were rushing to the nearest sanctuary. Weisman discovered that more Christians than Jews had crammed into his synagogue. In those dramatic days, there was much talk about a need to straighten out one's relationship with God. Mushy theologoumena went out of fashion. Liberal congregations cleaned up their act. In Washington D.C., two prominent churches, one Methodist, one Presbyterian, rolled in the huge flags in the rainbow colors—the banner of the homosexual lobby—that had adorned the exterior of these houses of worship.

But three months later, the Barna Research Group published disturbing results of an opinion poll. Diane Knippers, president of the Institute on Religion and Democracy and author of a stirring essay in this collection, told me she found Barna's findings scary. They revealed that only 22 percent of the American public—a little more than half as many as two years earlier—still believe in absolute moral truth. The Baby Buster generation gave Barna's pollsters even more alarming answers. A mere 13 percent of those young Americans aged 18 to 36 think that any absolute values exist. As Diane Knippers correctly stated, "This means that within another generation we may end up with a society that has abandoned the basic assumptions of democracy, assumptions such as human dignity and human freedom."

It is precisely this concern that makes the present collection of essays on Christ in postmodernity so urgent. The authors come from different traditions: several are Lutheran, others are evangelical, Roman Catholic, Episcopalian, Reformed, Pentecostal, or Byzantine. But the contributors have one thing in common: their faith in the very agent of creation who made Himself small, became a man, suffered and died "for me," as Martin Luther so crisply phrased it. There are theologians and journalists among the authors, as well as a manufacturer of farm implements, a scientist, a student, and an artist. What unites these authors is their agreement on Christ as the remedy against the chaos that threatens a new epoch that seems to confirm André Malraux's forecast that the third millennium would be "either a religious one or none at all." In other words, without a return to faith, there would not be another millennium for humanity.

Malraux, the French writer-politician, did not specify in what sense the millennium we have just entered would be religious. But September 11 has surfaced the significance of faith—for better or for worse. The terrorists who piloted hijacked planes into skyscrapers did so not out of atheistic or agnostic fervor. Indeed, had they been atheists—that is, materialists—they would presumably not have volunteered for a mission that would lead to their own material oblivion. Instead, these men went to their death in the name of their god, and they did so expecting to be rewarded in the afterlife.

Thus Malraux's words have proved prophetic. This is further underscored by the fact that the world's two largest monotheistic religions, Christianity and Islam, are growing robustly. It is ironic, however, that this occurs at a time when, at least in the West, the noisiest culture rejects the claims of these religions to absolute truth and moral standards. Adherents of this "noisy culture" do not deny the existence of a Creator, especially not in the United States, where poll after poll confirms that well over 90 percent of respondents believe in some sort of a deity. But is this deity the God of Scripture? Should He and His will be taken seriously? Evidently not because Barna's research has shown that an individual's faith has little effect on his or her moral choices. Perhaps more disconcerting, Barna's results reveal that Americans are "comfortable" legalizing even those actions they consider immoral, such as abortion, homosexuality, and pornography.

In our postmodern times, we are told that everybody may set his or her own truth or value, divorced from divine revelation, detached from God's Law and the natural law that He has written on every heart, to quote St. Paul. The result can only be chaos on an unprecedented scale. But to Christians, chaos is contrary to the will of God. It is satanic in the sense that it returns the universe to the state that existed prior to creation; it undoes God's work. This is the root of the "culture of death" that Pope John Paul II never tires of castigating. One can argue that Stalin, Hitler, and Mao were the progenitors of this lethal culture because they taught the world that there is nothing objectionable about lowering moral standards. We have seen the results, however: global bedlam accompanied by mass murder.

Postmodernists are heirs especially to Hitler because they discard rationalism, again with deadly consequences. The mass slaughter of unborn life that has occurred since Roe v. Wade in 1973 is a quintessentially postmodern phenomenon because it puts the momentary "need" of the self above the will of the Creator, whom postmodernity has reduced to the hapless state of a constitutional monarch of sorts.

Apart from that, postmodern irrationality has treated the world to the spectacle of incredible follies: educated people who commit mass suicide so their souls may be picked up by a passing spaceship that will take them to a better world; learned men and women in the Japanese Aum Shinrikyo sect who believe themselves called to trigger the Battle of Armageddon so everything will be made anew; and let's not forget the folly of Harvard lecturer Timothy Leary. He taught a generation of young Americans the use of the drug LSD as a substitute for God. When Leary was last heard of, his ashes were orbiting the planet in a capsule shot into space at his request.

It is ironic that postmodernity's diffuse properties also give us cause for hope. Bidding farewell to scientific rationalism, postmodern humanity has opened itself once again to beliefs that cannot be proven scientifically, for example, the belief in the incarnation of the logos. It is this truth that leading Christian thinkers identify as an antidote to postmodern chaos. This core Christian belief holds that the person of the Trinity who became incarnate in Jesus was the executor of creation (John 1:3)—and still is because creation is a continuing process.

Therefore, Christians posit the very one who structures the universe—the logos—against the postmodern folly that produces the opposite, chaos. This is why the editors of the UPI series and this collection of essays have ordered them thematically to loosely follow the church year from Advent to Christmas, from Lent to Easter, and on to Pentecost and Trinity.

There is a reason why the Christian church has followed this calendar for almost 2,000 years. This reason is not saccharine religious sentimentality, such as is pleasing to postmoderns. This is not about candles, poinsettias, Christmas trees, Easter eggs and bonnets, though none of these pleasant trimmings of Christian feasts deserve ridicule. The church year reminds us of a succession of events that stress the victory of divine order over chaos, of life over death, of truth over bogus truths. Taken together, these events constitute a magnificent drama of cosmic proportions, a perennial witness to the Word who became flesh and lived among us, the "One and Only, who came from the Father, full of grace and truth" (John 1:14 NIV). In this volume this drama is told in glimpses from various perspectives, all of which share a commitment to Christ.

~~~~

Dr. Uwe Siemon-Netto, a Lutheran lay theologian, is religion editor of United Press International in Washington, D.C.

ADVENT:
CHRIST VS. "TRUTHS"

GENE EDWARD VEITH

A s the season of Advent marks for Christians the beginning of a new church year in the third millennium, it is
clear that Christianity has outlived most of its critics. Many
pundits a hundred years ago predicted that religion would
die out in the twentieth century and would be replaced by
the modern age of science and reason.

Now the age of science and reason is under attack. The
new postmodern ways of thinking call rationalism itself into
question. Although postmodernism also poses challenges for
Christianity, challenges far different than those posed by
modernism, it is evident that Christ is more culturally relevant than ever.

Two thousand years after Christ, as we enter a new
century and a new cultural moment, we are still in the "year
of the Lord." The last century saw the rise of modern art,
modern literature, modern architecture, modern thought,
and modern theology, all grounded in the conviction that
the twentieth century was the culmination of scientific

progress and that old ways of thinking had to be cast out in favor of anything new.

It is ironic that, from the vantage point of the twenty-first century, all those "modernist" styles and ideas now seem old-fashioned, naïve, and culturally irrelevant. We are "post-modern," and in field after field the verities of modernism are collapsing like the Berlin Wall. The conquest of nature has given way to environmentalism. Abstract art is being replaced by concrete art. The desire for unity is now a desire for diversity. The hard sciences are bowing to the social sciences, which insist that culture, not nature, is the source of everything we can know. Technology continues to advance, but its focus has shifted from the manufacture of tangible goods to the manufacture of information.

In the last century, the principles of modern science were thought to be transferable to social problems so rationalistic ideologies and social experts could engineer a progressive utopia. The unintended consequences were concentration camps, gulags, world wars, and cold wars. Even the more benign welfare state solutions proved costly failures.

Somehow the new, unfettered information economy has brought a level of prosperity that all the rational systems never could. Observers in the 1890s, looking to the bright century ahead, predicted that in the twentieth century religion would die out. The modern mind, it was said, was ruled only by science. There would be no place for the supernatural, for what could not be empirically verified or rationally proven.

Many churches and their theologians, afraid of becoming culturally irrelevant, responded with a new, progressive, "modern" theology. The supernatural claims of Christianity were jettisoned, the Bible was demythologized, and salvation was turned into an allegory for the real work of the church, namely, improving society.

Ironically, the mainline churches that embraced modernist theology have themselves become culturally irrelevant. Far from dying out, religion of the most supernatural kind is booming, from megachurches with membership in the thousands to the most esoteric New Age mysticism. Even those who are not "religious" claim to be "spiritual."

Not that the twenty-first century is shaping up to be the utopia that the twentieth century failed to create. For all the economic boom of recent years, society is plagued by fragmentation, a lack of consensus on just about anything, and family breakdowns. Individuals often seem almost paralyzed by cynicism, indecision, and malaise.

There are basically two ways to respond to the end of modernity. One way of being postmodern is postmodernism, the new critical stance toward all knowledge that has found its way out of academia and into the popular culture. Just as modernism was marked by skepticism of everything not provable by scientific reasoning, postmodernism takes the next step: being skeptical of rationalism itself. For academic postmodernists, truth is not something we discover; rather, it is something we construct. Knowledge and morality, laws and institutions, the arts and the sciences are social constructions. There are no absolute truths, only a series of explanatory paradigms that have a pragmatic use but that vary from culture to culture.

Some postmodernists stress how truth claims and cultural institutions are essentially acts of power, the results of people in charge imposing their will through a façade of rationality or high moral purpose on groups they are oppressing (minorities, women, the poor, the homosexual, or other "marginalized" groups). Others stress that human beings can create their own truths by their own will. What may be true for one person may not be true for someone else, and no one has the right to impose his or her view on anyone else. For example, those who believe in abortion call themselves "pro-choice." According to postmodernist ethics, if a woman chooses to have the baby, that is right for her. If she chooses to have an abortion, that is right for her. The content of the decision—reference to any transcendent moral absolutes of right and wrong, or any objective information about the nature of the fetus or ethical arguments—has no bearing. Having a choice is what gives the action moral validity. Postmodernist ethics are also evident in debates about euthanasia (If a person chooses to die, how can we say no?) and genetic engineering (Parents should be able to choose the kind of baby they want).

Popular postmodernism is evident in the recent U.S. election debacle. Modernists assumed that it was possible to hold an election by ascertaining an objective, mathematical count, a process helped by the inexorable objectivity of machines. But in our first postmodern election, objective certainty was thrown into doubt. The findings of voting machines were suspect, and the machines were replaced by human observers who interpreted the significance of tiny indentations or hanging chad on pieces of paper. For postmodernists, all meaning is nothing more than interpretation, and interpretation is inherently subjective, variable from one person to another, and open to ideological bias.

Whether Western democracies built on earlier worldviews that affirmed objective truth and transcultural absolutes can survive postmodernist skepticism remains to be seen. But there is another way to respond to the end of modernity, another way to be postmodern. Instead of extending the critical spirit of modernity to reason itself, another option is to recover the premodern, to bring back the insights and achievements of the past and apply them, in new ways, to the contemporary condition.

This, too, is happening throughout the culture. Contemporary artists are experimenting in new ways with classical aesthetics. New homes have Victorian-era gables, wraparound porches, and other retro-stylings, with the addition of all of the high-tech conveniences. Historical novels and movies are in vogue. Educators are rediscovering classical education as a better way to teach in the computer age. And millions of lives are being changed by historic, conservative Christianity as nearly every denomination is rediscovering its distinct confessional and spiritual heritage.

To be sure, many churches, emulating the modernist theologians of the last century, are changing their teachings and practices to fit the tenets of postmodernism. Some are jettisoning their doctrines, allowing each member to construct his or her own beliefs. Some are playing down their traditional moral teachings, cultivating the postmodern virtue of "tolerance" for all lifestyle choices.

If modernist churches promoted an ecumenism that attempted to bring all Christian churches into unity, postmodernist ecumenism embraces all religions, promoting a syncretic universalism (mixing religions) that believes all faiths are equally valid paths to God. Even churches that maintain a veneer of conservatism are flirting with postmodernism. If beliefs are only consumer choices, persuasion—whether in sales, politics, or religion—becomes a matter of marketing, of manipulating customers by the cultivation of image and by "meeting the consumers' needs." Thus the mass-marketing techniques perfected by the new economy are being used by many churches to mutate into megachurches, which appeal to a mass market through entertainment-style worship and positive thinking ("you create your own reality") sermons.

Yet at the same time, in a passionate response to the end of modernity, other churches and other Christians are rediscovering ancient liturgies and ancient theologies. The practices and beliefs of the early church, the insights of the Protestant Reformation, the witness of persecuted Christians, indeed all examples of the faith practiced in the face of

cultural hostility and cultural change, seem uncannily relevant today. And faith in the one who is the Alpha and the
Omega, the beginning and the end, and who brought salvation not by setting up an earthly utopia but by dying on a
cross seems to be girding itself for another thousand years.

~~~~~

Dr. Gene Edward Veith Jr. is professor of English at
Concordia University Wisconsin. His book *Postmodern
Times* (Crossway, 1994) was the first major attempt to
analyze this new era from a Christian perspective.

GENDER PEACE
THROUGH CHRIST

SARAH HINLICKY

Men are inherently offensive to women. It starts before kindergarten when we first notice their passion for belching and public nose-picking.

The offense swells as we grow up together. The boys drop out of our games of peace—from the domestic peace of dolls and dress-up to the creative peace of threads, beads, and paints, the completion of peaceful projects that construct a lovelier world. They, we note with not a little disdain, turn to trucks and guns and "action figures" (decidedly not dolls). They slam one another into the mud during their impromptu games of football, bearing their scabs from failed skateboarding stunts like personal purple hearts. Boys are noisy, violent, grubby, gross.

The offense hardly lessens when, with adulthood, men turn to work, ideas, and projects—and all too many times prefer them to us.

Some of us claim that women have had little opportunity to exercise the vice of pride in our lives. We have, it is said, been too downtrodden to think so well of ourselves. But the claim righteously made against our suppression conceals a dirty secret: Our creeping sense of spiritual superiority has exacerbated the war between us and them.

Funny how we have exploited the achievements of the past hundred years since negotiating a peace treaty to trespass the bounds of justice into the tastier realm of vengeance. How we love to punish men for being men. We are crafty—craftier than they have given us credit for in recent memory. We have wrested away their unthinking masculinity to redefine it by our own vicious formula: Men (real men, unreformed men, natural men) are cruel, men are promiscuous, men are authoritarian. How earnestly we desire to remake men in our own image.

As women we always suspect that we deserve something better, men who do not want to possess and protect but listen and sympathize; men who do not (alas, the frustrating contradiction) command with one breath and lay down their lives with the next. Men in their crassness and silly toughness ought never to insinuate, however unconsciously, however innocently, that we women are not the complete picture of humanity.

It implicates our abstinence of the soul. We teach men well that their purity can never match ours, and, understandably, they cease to try. So our dignity looks down, down an infinite distance, to our males below, in all their canine enthusiasms and leonine ferocities. We pretend to ourselves through our friendships and dates and affairs and marriages and divorces that we really are engaging the male, but for all our engagement, we quietly refuse to grant men their humanity. We, the peacemakers, have learned the subtle art of making war.

Into this life of calm and gentle judgment strides the God who became man. And not just man in the grandly generic and, therefore, safe sense but man, a man, not a woman. This God-man cannot save women, some of us have said. The God that does not look like me cannot uplift me. The God that does not suffer like me cannot redeem me. And do we, therefore, ignore His helpless cries from the manger? Do the baby's tears go uncomforted because the baby is a boy? Is this God too lowly for us, too ridiculous for having invaded the world by way of a womb? It is a possibility. We're tempted to reject motherhood because the God-man has tainted it.

There is plenty we must reject to be consistently free of the God-man's interference. We must do away with the hospitality practiced by Martha, do away with the contemplative discipleship of her sister, Mary. We must not learn to worship in spirit and truth like the woman at the well. We must not love so much and thereby abase ourselves so much that we cleanse and kiss and perfume the feet of another.

We must never prophesy, never pray, never labor like Phoebe the deacon nor evangelize like Priscilla. Silence, fortitude, autonomy, perfect self-belonging must be ours if we are to escape the reaching, shaping hands of the man who is God, who presumes to desire us in service with those men whose potential for godliness we are compelled respectfully to doubt.

Can it be that the God-man, in fact, redeems unredeemable men? He promises to make men who love us as much as He loves the church. He pledges to teach men to nourish and care as tenderly for us as they do their own bodies. He will lead them (so He says) to sacrifice everything for us. He insists upon redefining masculinity against our own redefinition—and then reserving its practice for men alone. Dare we contemplate something so unjust?

Here we find ourselves facing the unthinkable. The God-man trumpets into our pure, boxed-in lives that there is something liberating about allowing men to be with us and not beneath us. He proclaims that there is joy in discovering a man to whom we can submit, yet still be free. He declares that there is something essentially good about men being men. Is our femininity strong enough to face it, or have we been hiding something faulty in ourselves? Can it be (scandalous thought) that we are as helpless without men as they are without us? Can it be that the God-man both exposes and heals our failure to love men as men and, finally, creates the peace that we have craved from the start? Can it be that our femininity itself is in need of redemption?

The mother of God sings in the Magnificat, perhaps the most beautiful and radical hymn in Scripture:

> My soul magnifies the Lord . . . for He has regarded the low estate of His handmaiden. For behold, henceforth all generations will call me blessed . . . . He has scattered the proud in the imagination of their hearts . . . and exalted those of low degree. (Luke 1:46–52 RSV)

God comes to a woman and through her the God-man comes to the world. Born of this woman, Jesus inaugurates and extends His reign of peace. But where is the imagination of her heart? And will she cling to her seat on the throne?

~~~~

Sarah Hinlicky is a student at Princeton Theological Seminary.

THE PROMISE
OF COSMIC PEACE

TED PETERS

One of the marks of postmodernity is intellectual chaos. To a theologian dabbling in cosmology, this poses a set of questions: Can there be a world-ordering mind of God? Is there a world order of any type that the human mind can understand? At Christmastime, we look at the baby in the Bethlehem manger and wonder, Does it make sense to say: He is the incarnation of the divine logos, the God "through [whom] all things were made" (John 1:3 NIV)?

Two types of postmodern cosmology are fighting for our allegiance: the deconstructionist and the holistic. The former is the child of Martin Heidegger's philosophy and literary criticism. Heidegger (1889–1976) was a German philosopher between the world wars of the twentieth century. He said he wanted to "rethink being" as we inherited it from Plato (428–348 B.C.). Being isn't what it used to be, or so it seems.

For nearly three centuries, literary criticism has treated the Bible as if it is one piece of literature among others, looking at the human perspective rather than claims that this book is divine or absolute. With Heidegger's philosophy and with literary criticism as its parents, postmodernity considers claims about ultimate reality as a text to be analyzed. For this purpose the text is to be reduced, or deconstructed, to the author's perspective.

This is what we call relativism, and it is relativism with a vengeance. No longer can we rely upon reason to connect us with reality. No longer are claims to understand ultimate or universal reality self-evident. Deconstructionism dismisses each scientific or metaphysical claim about nature as just one more social construction. It reinterprets all rational claims about our cosmic home—whether scientific or religious—as mere ideological projections of our need to protect the social dominance of one class over another.

Holistic postmodernism, in contrast, perceives an underlying unity to all things, a semimystical glue that binds it all together. Everything in this glorious cosmos, from soul to stars, is interrelated, connected, shared. Both science and spirituality lift up this awareness, which is empowering to the human spirit. Curiously, Heidegger's philosophy is a grandparent here, too, because it emphasizes that human meaning is defined by connectedness and relatedness. Heidegger's thought mates with New Age mysticism to produce a holistic child with an ecological vision of unity between body and spirit, mind and world, humanity and nature.

What we have is a postmodern intellectual war. Into this war the Christmas voice of the Gospel of John whispers: "The Word was made flesh" (John 1:14 KJV). The Word here is the Word of God. It is the same Word we heard in Genesis when God speaks and out of nothing all of reality springs into being. This is the same Word we find on Mount Sinai when Moses brought down the Ten Commandments. This is the same Word by which the cosmos is ordered according to the divine mind and the divine will.

Over the centuries we learned of this Word by reading two books. The first book is the Book of Nature, which is read by scientific experimentation. In this book the divine mind is displayed in the amazing configuration of mathematical laws that govern our physical universe. Plato read the human mind and discovered the numbers that make for harmony in nature, as well as in music. Plato's student, Aristotle (A.D. 384–322), read the plants and animals and discovered the organization of life. Galileo read the moons of Jupiter through his telescope. Sir Isaac Newton (1647–1727) read the laws of motion that kept those moons of Jupiter in orbit. Albert Einstein (1879–1955) read the relationship between matter and energy and did the math, remarking that "God does not play dice with the universe."

I once spoke with a Hindu physicist about this. I asked him whether he tended toward a more personal or impersonal understanding of the divine Brahman, the creator in Hinduism's trinity. "Oh, I believe I need to think of God as personal," he said. Then he continued, "When I view the awesome glory of those 50 billion galaxies strewn throughout this magnificent cosmos, when I look in the cloud chambers at the paths of those unpredictable electrons, and when I see how mathematical laws unite such an otherwise unfathomable array of natural phenomena with such elegance and beauty, I just want to say 'thank you' to someone."

The second book tells us whom to thank. This is the Book of Revelation, not only the last book of the Bible, but the whole Bible, wherein God's promise for the future new creation is delivered to human ears who are ready to hear it. This promise is found in the prophets, who look forward to a time when the lion will lie down with the lamb. The promise is found in visions of the new Jerusalem in which the river of life we left in the Garden of Eden now runs through the downtown park of the heavenly city.

All this symbolic language directs our gaze toward a reality that is promised but not yet here. It points to the reality that became flesh in ancient Israel, a fleshly reality that the world could not tolerate, so it resorted to crucifixion. God confirmed this reality when He raised the crucified Christ—the Word—from the dead on the first Easter and promised that the whole cosmos would in the future get its Easter too.

The idea of the two books leads us to treat nature as a text almost like we treat the Bible as a text. In both cases we're looking for the author's point of view, the author's social location.

Just who is the author? The scribes who took quill in hand and placed ink on vellum? Yes, but that's not all. God is speaking in, with, and under what is human and ideological, and He gives a perspective to the biblical text. The Swiss theologian Karl Barth (1886–1968) used to say that the Bible is the divine Word in human words. Something parallel happens when we treat nature as a book. It takes place when we ask our scientific researchers to help us understand the language of nature so we, in turn, can ask about its transcendent author—the one who utters the divine Word.

When this Word becomes flesh in that Bethlehem manger, the Prince of Peace has come for a visit. The order of God is finally the order of peace. The promise of new creation embodied in the Prince of Peace is the divine promise that the laws of nature are aiming toward peace in the cosmos. And the promise of cosmic peace translates into our mandate to work toward that peace on our planet, to bring peace on earth. The present creation strains after the new creation, where we will find peace even between deconstructionist and holistic postmodernists.

~~~~~

The Rev. Dr. Ted Peters is professor of systematic theology at Pacific Lutheran Theological Seminary and program director at the Center for Theology and the Natural Sciences at Berkeley.

CHRISTMAS: THE BIRTH OF A JEWISH BABE

DAVID BRICKNER

Everyone missed the most significant news event of the year, except for a few shepherds, a couple of elderly folks in Jerusalem, and several political leaders from the Far East. The news? A Jewish girl had given birth to a baby boy and placed Him in a manger in Bethlehem. Hardly headline news—except for the fact that this baby boy would change the course of human history. Except for the fact that the birth of this child would signal world redemption. Except for the fact that this birth in that backwater town would become the moment by which all other events in time would be measured for both Jews and Gentiles.

It is easy to understand how most of humanity missed the event. People tend to be impressed by all that appears big and powerful. We are captivated by the trite and titillated by the trendy. But the machinations of the politically powerful do not set the course of history any more than the trends of popular culture do. Those who try to read the signs of the times through the postmodern lens of popular culture will miss it every time. So what qualities enabled a select few to recognize the really important thing God was doing in Bethlehem?

Those first-century shepherds on the hills outside Bethlehem were a simple and lowly folk. (Shepherding was often reserved for the youngest member of a family. If an adult was given the task, it was not because he had an excellent resume.) To these shepherds, the revelation of the babe came and the glory of God was revealed. Perhaps their willingness to let the truth be the truth and to respond without rationalization made them the most likely candidates to hear from God.

"Though the LORD is on high, He looks upon the lowly, but the proud He knows from afar" (Psalm 138:6 NIV). Also "The LORD preserves the simple" (Psalm 116:6 RSV). Our savvy and sophisticated culture prefers cynicism to simplicity. The "wise" of our day would have us believe that issues of truth and morality are much too complicated to be known. And the more complex something appears— the more indecipherable—the more appealing it is to many.

But with God it's different. If we want to be among those who recognize His hand in history, it's necessary to resist cynical tendencies in ourselves and in our society. It is necessary to prefer simple truth to complex sophistry and to view the trends of our postmodern culture through the lens and light of God's revelation. In this way we can quiet the din of worldly clamor and listen for the voices of angels.

The Christmas carols identify the second group who saw what God was doing in their time as "kings of Orient," but the Bible calls them "Magi" or "Wise Men." They were diviners of signs and stars, schooled in reading and interpreting the ancient texts. They were not kings but advisers to kings, politicians of a religious stripe. And these particular political leaders from the East were truly seeking God.

Today many people seek spiritual enlightenment from the comfort of their own living rooms. They can tune in to the latest popular preacher with their television remote control or surf the eclectic spiritual galaxy with the click of a computer mouse. But what does it really mean to seek after God? Truly seeking after God involves devotion, a determination that requires the seeker to set aside comfort and convention, to pursue with abandon the one who alone is mighty to save.

Something within those Wise Men led them from the comfort and safety of their prominent positions to make the long journey to a foreign land. When they found Him whom they sought, not in a palace but in a tiny impoverished Jewish town, they were not disappointed. They worshiped Him and gave gifts. And they were able to partake in God's messianic promise, though they were outsiders: "You will seek Me and find Me when you seek Me with all your heart" (Jeremiah 29:13 NIV).

The third group able to recognize what God was doing in their time were saintly sages, two elderly Jewish folk whose hearts were attuned to the promises of the Scriptures. Anna was a prophetess. Simeon was "waiting for the consolation of Israel" (Luke 2:25 NIV). Together they represented those who studied the Bible and believed it to be absolutely true and trustworthy. They knew that human destiny was not dependent on the power of the sword or political manipulation but on the sovereign plan of God. They understood that this plan would be entrusted to a baby boy.

This was God's way. Simeon said, "Behold, this child is set for the fall and rising of many in Israel, and for a sign that is spoken against" (Luke 2:34 RSV). When we understand the Scriptures, when our hopes and our dreams are rooted in the Word of God, neither appearances nor outward circumstances will sway us. Thus Simeon and Anna held in their very arms the one who would redeem Israel and be "a light for revelation to the Gentiles" as well.

How surprising that the God of Israel should choose to reveal His Son's arrival to these three different groups. Yet in a sense, the Messiah was much like those to whom His advent was first revealed. He came as a lowly shepherd, one who was not esteemed but who faithfully cared for those in His charge. Like the Magi, He journeyed far from a high position to present Himself in a humble place. And like Anna and Simeon, He knew all the promises of God and was born for that very purpose.

People from any background today can still seek and find Him if they will follow the example of those who searched and found Him so very long ago.

~~~~~

The Rev. David Brickner is the executive director of Jews for Jesus.

POSTMODERNITY'S INNOCENT SAINTS

DIANE KNIPPERS

Oddly nestled between the joyous celebration of Christmas and the revelry of New Year's Eve is a Christian holy day that marks a dreadful event. It is the Feast of the Holy Innocents, which commemorates the "massacre of the innocents"—an attempt by a wicked king to rid himself of a presumed threat to his sovereignty.

Perhaps understandably we often omit this gruesome tale in our repetitions of the Christmas story. Our nativity scenes—filled with the infant Jesus and His parents, gentle animals, wondering shepherds, generous Wise Men, stars, and angels—do not include Roman soldiers eviscerating babies. Besides, what does this tale of ancient Roman brutality have to do with us as we march boldly into a new year early in a new millennium? Perhaps more than we care to admit.

The terrible story is told in the second chapter of Matthew. At the time Jesus was born, Magi, or "wise men from the East," noted an unusual astrological event. Taking this as a sign, they traveled westward to Palestine, seeking the "king of the Jews." Not surprisingly, the travelers went first to the Jewish holy city of Jerusalem. From there, they were directed a few miles south, to Bethlehem, from whence, according to prophecy, the Messiah was to come.

Tragically, their stop in Jerusalem alerted the paranoid King Herod to their quest. Herod was not a Jew. The Roman Senate had appointed him King of Judea. His reign was noted for its splendid building campaigns. It was also noted for its ruthlessness. Among those Herod had murdered were his wife and three sons. For Herod, power was the end that justified any means. He instructed the Magi to search for the new baby king. He asked them to report back to him "so that I too may go and worship Him" (Matthew 2:8 NIV). The Magi were successful in finding the infant Jesus. But the Gospel tells that they were warned of Herod's duplicity in a dream and took another route home.

Similarly, in a dream an angel instructed Jesus' parents to flee with Him to Egypt. Then came the horror: "When Herod realized that he had been outwitted by the Magi, he was furious, and he gave orders to kill all the boys in Bethlehem and its vicinity who were two years old and under" (Matthew 2:16 NIV). Matthew does not give a count of how many youngsters were killed. The narrative asserts only that Jeremiah's prophecy was fulfilled: "A voice is heard in Ramah, weeping and great mourning, Rachel weeping for her children and refusing to be comforted, because they are no more" (Matthew 2:18 [NIV], quoting Jeremiah 31:15).

There are places today where mothers mourn their missing children. Too often the lives of innocent children are sacrificed to the political plans of the powerful. The blood may not run in the streets, and the mothers may be counseled to stifle their unseemly wailing, but the numbers who silently perish are all the greater.

In Bethlehem, a few years after the massacre, perhaps only the demographics would have hinted at the horror that had occurred. A naïve visitor might have asked, "Why are there so few little boys?" Five years ago while visiting China, my impressions confirmed the grim demographics of that nation. I saw more boys than girls. Why the discrepancy? It was a confluence of the state's "one child policy" and the traditional Chinese preference for boys. Little girls are expendable. They are aborted by the millions.

In the United States we do not target baby girls as they do in China, but the logic that drives the abortion industry here is similar. The babies who die are the ones who are "not wanted." They are the ones who do not fit with the expectations and plans of their parents and society. Their continued existence would be a challenge to the claimed sovereignty of a woman over her own body. And the unborn children often lose that challenge because they are powerless and innocent.

The logic of Herod also operates in many current political conflicts. In Sudan the government uses food as a weapon of war, stopping deliveries of food to rebel-controlled areas. This policy is estimated to have produced two million deaths in the past 20 years. Most of the dead are children, who succumb more quickly when nutrition is lacking. The government in Khartoum is more concerned with vindicating its claims to sovereignty.

The analogy between Herod and modern rulers is disturbingly comprehensible. Herod's carefully targeted killings can't be dismissed as an emotional overreaction that epitomizes ancient Roman extravagance and decadence. No, they were highly logical acts, illustrative of modern rationalism. Herod killed only boys, only those two years old and younger, only those living near Bethlehem. The modern era has seen such carefully calibrated massacres as well: The Communists marked the bourgeoisie and the church. The Nazis performed their precise scientific experiments on the handicapped, then employed efficient technology to kill millions of Jews.

The scientific rationality of modernity allows us to make calculated decisions about who lives and who dies. As the techniques of genetic analysis become more sophisticated, we may see abortions targeted even more specifically at the "undesirables." In a few decades perhaps a visitor to the United States might ask, "Why are your children all so light-skinned? Why are they all so tall and nimble-minded?"

As we have moved into the twenty-first century, modernism has given way to postmodernism. In part the move is a reaction to the cold computations of scientific rationalism. Postmodernism leaves room for spirituality and for intuition. Postmodernism resists the rational calculation of which lives are "worthy" to be lived. But will postmodernism save the babies?

Postmodernism's fatal flaw is moral relativism. "Don't impose your rigid ethics on me," we protest. "I'm inventing my own identity," we boast. "I'm the sovereign of my own life" is our new postmodern commandment. I can hear wily old Herod pontificating, "What matters is what's right for me." He would still have the power to command the slaughter, and his postmodern subjects would lack the moral fortitude to resist.

Neither modernism nor postmodernism will protect the babies. Two thousand years later, the best hope for the little ones is the other Baby from Bethlehem. Contrary to Herod's expectations, Jesus did not come to claim a throne by force. He did not compel others to yield to His sovereignty. Instead, He "came not to be served but to serve, and to give His life as a ransom for many" (Mark 10:45 RSV).

Having escaped Herod's massacre of the innocents, Jesus later offered His own life as the ultimate innocent victim of human ambition and jealousy. Jesus' resurrection from the dead opened the alternative to the "culture of death" represented by Herod and his modern equivalents. Jesus promised abundant life to all, especially to the powerless and the oppressed. And He proclaimed this with an extraordinary authority and conviction of the truth: "I am the way and the truth and the life" (John 14:6 NIV). This assurance can give Jesus' followers courage to challenge every false, life-suppressing claim to sovereignty—ancient, modern, or postmodern.

The Feast of the Holy Innocents is a grim specter at a birthday party. It confronts us with the evil of which we humans are capable. It reminds us that Jesus was born to die. It portends the shadow of the cross. It enjoins us to celebrate Christmas with more than saccharine songs to the famous Babe of Bethlehem. That Baby would have us remember all the other unwanted but precious babies in Bethlehem and in our towns.

~~~~

Diane Knippers is president of the Institute on Religion and Democracy in Washington, D.C.

A FLEET
IN POSTMODERN GALES

WILLIAM G. RUSCH

One of the most ancient images of the church is that of a ship. This depiction has been found in the catacombs around Rome, on funerary steles and gems of the late Roman Empire, and in the literary remains of the early church. Already in the second century, Justin Martyr, a church leader and theologian in Gaul, wrote of the church as a ship journeying on the waters of life, steered by Christ, and transporting a cargo of human souls to salvation. It is certainly accurate to assume that Justin is reflecting an oral teaching of the church that is much older than his writings.

The symbolism of the church as a ship is easy to grasp. Christ called His followers from their fishing boats. He personally taught from these boats. The cross-rigging of a mast can easily be viewed as a cross. The journey of a ship across perilous seas becomes a description of the believer's course through life with the assurance that Christ is the helmsman who brings the vessel to the final port of eternal salvation.

This portrayal has continuing validity. It is useful to observe the church across the centuries as a ship. In its earliest days, the church was not only buffeted by the strong winds of Hellenism and the intellectual breezes of the late Roman Empire, but it acquired direction in these wings of wind. In medieval Europe this skiff discovered comfort in the airy currents of Aristotelian thought rediscovered by the scholastics. The vessel soon found itself in the crosswinds of the Reformation, which while not submerging the craft, at least in terms of the image saw the stately ship transformed into a fleet of smaller ships, uncertain as to whether or not they sailed under the same flag.

This flotilla experienced the cutting gales of the Enlightenment, which to this day have left deep scars and caused the church to question its course of travel. Most recently these ecclesiastical barks have encountered the squalls of twentieth-century modernity. In these tempestuous blasts, the ships have struggled to remain on course as the traditional values of family, community, and even the church as institution have bent or snapped in the wind.

Under the perceived pressure to survive, a sense of the transcendent, the uniqueness of the Bible, and an understanding of salvation as anything other than an improvement of society were cast overboard. Rationalism, secularism, and a supreme confidence in science were welcomed as shipmates. Yet as these scolding winds moved away, the resulting attitude of those sailing on all the vessels was one of cynicism, indecision, and malaise.

A new squall line appeared on the horizon as if in reaction to the downdraft of modernity. This phenomenon was actually a constellation of countergales. It was an indeterminate collection of crosswinds, without beginning or end. It pummeled these ships. Although this phenomenon was described as postmodernity, there is no single entity that can be so delineated. One thing this confluence of winds and currents shared, which distinguished it from modernity, was an absolute pessimism.

The buffeting turbulence of postmodernity swept away confidence in rational thought, the virtues of secularism, and the superiority of science. If it appeared at one time that modernity had provided a compass so the ecclesial fleet could navigate in strange, even hostile, waters, the blasts of postmodernity carried away such devices. For a foundering flotilla, there now seemed to be no absolute truths, no transcendent values, and no morality. All these deep issues of life became something individuals construct at their own whim.

But is the good fleet called church really without a rudder in such dirty seas and howling winds? Numerous answers have been given to this cutting question. Responses range from a simplistic yearning for the carefree waters of yesteryear, which never actually existed, to a state of near despair, and on to a creative grappling with the contemporary situation. The simplistic yearning finds expression in fundamentalism or evangelicalism—both of which seek to avoid or ignore the squalls of modernity and postmodernity.

The state of despair, not without some reason, at least uncovers an explanation for the listing of the ships in the fact that God causes storms. It raises the fearful prospect that God has abandoned this group of ships called church. These vessels are buffeted by other winds than the breath of the Spirit because God has so determined. This is a frightening possibility that cannot be probed in depth here. Yet such a state of despair cannot be nonchalantly dismissed. Evidence of previous similar experiences is found in the pages of Scripture, and serious voices, even if with some tentativeness, make the suggestion at the present moment.

Without a final judgment on this sobering eventuality, there is a third choice for these ships. They possess ancient charts from both Testaments. They are entrusted with the promise of an ever-present pilot. The resources are there not for a mere repristination of history, but to recover the insights of a past that is indelibly marked by the triune God and to apply these insights to a new situation.

The new state of affairs is the possibility of a new configuration for the ecclesiastical ships of this fleet. So much of their history has been spent maneuvering in a context of real or apparent hostility—do they indeed sail under the same Captain? The ecumenical movement of the last century, with its deep desire for the visible unity of the church of Christ, has traveled a long distance in resolving this question. It has removed caricatures of the other vessels. It has brought increased communication between the ships. In the area of theology, it has interpreted differences and resulted in startling agreements.

This fleet should now sail together in greater harmony and cooperation toward its common home port. But severe debates rage on all these ships: Should the cargo of the ecumenical movement be taken on board and received into the hulls of these vessels? Could such freight be dangerous for the voyage, or is it an asset?

As this fragile flotilla sets course into the new millennium, it must ponder and resolve such questions because they will determine its final destination. Whether it moves beyond the whirlwinds of postmodernity to other seas will depend on numerous factors, many of which will lie not in its power but in the hands of that one who is Lord of winds and seas.

"The sea is His, for He made it . . ." (Psalm 95:5 NRSV)

"Then He got up and rebuked the winds and the sea; and there was a dead calm. They were amazed, saying, 'What sort of man is this, that even the winds and the sea obey Him?' " (Matthew 8:26–27 NRSV)

~~~~~

The Rev. Dr. William G. Rusch is executive director of the Foundation for a Conference on Faith and Order in North America.

CHRIST AND POSTMODERN RACIAL HARMONY

JOHN F. JOHNSON

As an African American pastor, I need to throw down the gauntlet right away. The thinking of white America has just caught up to the thinking of African Americans, who have been thinking postmodern for as long as I can remember.

Please understand, I'm not saying that postmodern thinking is healthy or good; I'm saying it simply "is" among African Americans. The key mark of postmodern thinking is that subjectivity is supreme. What a person feels, thinks, or perceives is the legitimate, primary source for all his or her decision-making. This ultimately, despite many apologists, is the reason why the African American community is plagued with crime, poverty, fatherless children, drugs, alcohol and tobacco addiction, endangered youth, and a preponderance of abortions.

Proverbs 29:18 says, "Where there is no revelation, the people cast off restraint; but blessed is he who keeps the law" (NIV). Regardless of the more common uses of this Scripture text by ministers, the real point is that unless the

Word of God is proclaimed, believed, and obeyed, the people will fall into self-destructive thinking and behavior.

Anyone can blame his troubles on outside forces, but in a quiet, clear moment he knows these troubles are his own fault. Therefore, from the biblical perspective, we have sought—and continue to seek—solutions for the African American community in the wrong places. Obedience to God's Word is the only solution for what ails the people.

I have had countless sessions with young African American men who argue that my "biblical advice" was a ploy to prevent them from experiencing life to the fullest. Because I was older and had experienced my fun, they alleged, I now wanted to use God to curb their opportunities for fun, romance, and everything else life has to offer. This honest reaction declares that truth, for these young men, is subjective. Even more telling is that postmodern thinking acknowledges what God says as useful but never ultimate. Therefore, for me as pastor to proclaim God's Word is simply to muddy the waters and add extra, but not definitive, data.

Scripture tells us: "Trust in the LORD with all your heart and lean not on your own understanding; in all your ways acknowledge Him, and He will make your paths straight. Do not be wise in your own eyes . . ." (Proverbs 3:5–7a NIV). This warning points out the fruitless nature of being a law unto yourself. We all need to acknowledge that there is only one absolute, objective truth to which all opinion and thinking must be subject.

Today in the African American community, Scripture is no longer the one absolute, objective truth. There are many competing truths that have various levels of merit. "But what of the Black church, the foundation of the African American community?" you ask. There are still plenty of churches in our communities, but most serve up Jesus Christ and Scripture cafeteria-style. Come on in and enjoy yourself! Try a little here and there, and swallow only what appeals to you. In an attempt to appeal to a wide variety of age groups and mind-sets in the African American community, we knowingly tiptoe around most of the Bible's absolutes. Then if we do happen to verbally endorse a few absolutes, they are never enforced when someone is bold enough to challenge them. This weakness in the church has led to a lifestyle that says, "I'm a Christian on Sunday, but the rest of the week belongs to me."

Unless Jesus Christ is truly presented as Lord of lords, as the one name under heaven by which we might be saved, and unless Scripture is our norm for believing and living, then no people, especially African Americans, can hope to function on any level of significance. Confused and aimless people are in no condition to reach out and grow in harmony with other races and people groups. Each race, mired in its own stupor, is prone to subjective generalizations concerning others—generalizations that exist based on mistrust, blame, and envy. This is our current dilemma in America. Confused, foundationless people are forced to make generalizations about other races and people groups. "You know how they are; they all act like that." These generalizations don't allow for true understanding or communication. They lead each group to feel misunderstood and to assume malice on the part of the other.

Because African Americans figured out postmodernity before everyone else, maybe we can likewise be the ones who again humble ourselves and heed the call of Jesus Christ so God might hear us and heal our land. God has plenty of room in His kingdom for all who put their trust in His one absolute, objective truth revealed in Christ. Only in Jesus will humanity's races find the ability to share respect, peace, and harmony.

~~~~~

The Rev. John F. Johnson is pastor of Mount Olivet Lutheran Church, Washington, D. C.

A BEACON
FOR
POSTMODERN POLITICS

HANS APEL

TRANSLATED BY UWE SIEMON-NETTO

An avowed Christian in the White House is fighting a war against global terrorism. This seems a proper occasion for a fellow Protestant and politician from an allied nation to reflect on this postmodern era with its chaotic profusion of homemade "truths." More than two decades ago, I was a West German government minister, first of finance, then of defense. I am a Social Democrat and have always considered myself a committed Lutheran.

A clergyman I much admired in my youth was Otto Dibelius, whom the Nazis had persecuted severely. After World War II he served as presiding bishop of Germany's territorial Protestant churches. Long before the war, Dibelius had predicted, "Whatever one might think of the Church, there can be no doubt that we are entering a century of the church." The bishop thought it impossible for the state and secularized society to survive without Christian guidance in the great ethical questions of life.

There were great hopes in 1945 and 1989 after first National Socialism and then Communism had collapsed. Europe anticipated a renaissance of the church and of basic Christian values in countries freed from terror. To be sure, these nations' democratic structures are solid now. Eventually they will be firmly anchored in the minds of a vast majority of Western Europeans; in the eastern part of the continent, this process will take a little longer.

Yet if you equate Christianity with our major churches, its anchor among the people seems to be cutting loose. Many are leaving their denominations. Even those still connected to their church seem less and less religiously committed. The result is spiritual impoverishment. Our Lord's message seems to evaporate in the everyday hustle and bustle. Once traditional Christian life has been emptied of meaning, it no longer keeps the individual in its grip.

Let's not fool ourselves: Many do not see this development as a loss; they feel liberated from what had seemed a burden to them. Now that we have moved into a new century, the old one does not seem a "century of the church" at all. Instead, it appears to have left the church behind, at least in Germany and much of Western Europe. The church, especially in its Protestant manifestations, seems trapped in the same quicksand that has sucked up mass movements that tried to eradicate humanity, human dignity, and individuality—movements symbolized by Auschwitz and the gulags.

After this historical experience, people in Europe no longer trust doctrines of salvation, including, alas, the teachings of Christianity. This being so, by which light should we now seek orientation for our journey through life? How are we to handle life's crises, such as unemployment, divorce, sickness, and death?

In Germany, the churches' past problem was that they had resisted meekly in the years of totalitarian violence and seemed more interested in their own preservation as institutions than in the inalienable rights of human beings. The churches' current problem tends to be that in these free and democratic times they are trying to make up for their deficits in the totalitarian past. Whether it is a protest against NATO, the peaceful use of nuclear energy, or the destruction of the environment, parts of the church will inevitably chime in. But in this participation, churches betray Christ's Great Commission to bring the Gospel to all people. Breathlessly, the churches chase after the *Zeitgeist*. And if you criticize such behavior by pointing to the New Testament, you will be belittled as a sectarian or a simple-minded idealist.

As a Lutheran, I am presumably beyond suspicion of being an excessive admirer of the papacy. Yet as I watch great Protestant denominations disintegrate theologically and observe their bishops kowtow to fads and betray their Lord, I can't help sympathizing with Roman order. Although "pluralism" seems to be today's mantra, what we really need is a plurality in the *unity* of faith. What we don't need is to see the Gospel melt away like a sugar cube in an ocean of temporal and societal "choices."

In Europe, as in North America, we discern the clouds of postmodernity's disintegrative might. Our political landscapes have changed dramatically. The great Christian Democratic parties are mere shadows of their former selves. Social Democracy, my political home for decades, has lost its identity. Once grandiose designs for a new societal beginning after World War II bound us together; this is no more. The young don't know what to make of these kinds of tradition. The parties have become geriatric clubs.

Occasionally, "Social Democrats" such as British Prime Minister Tony Blair and German Chancellor Gerhard Schröder still indulge in modernity's rituals, purporting "vision" and purpose. But in reality they are postmodernists. They are unprincipled opportunists without any commitment to an ultimate reality. They are muddling through, which provides for some temporary political success without any lasting moral effect. Ultimately, it won't benefit anybody.

Thus all presuppositions are crumbling. Modernity had at least tried to give meaning to life, but postmodernity has rendered this endeavor senseless. Old convictions and yesterday's truths are being questioned and reduced to ambiguity. Humanity tries to free itself of yesterday's constraints. The individual is striving for self-determination. According to opinion polls, "doing one's own thing" is the highest goal of young Germans, ages 16 to 27. In the poll's scale of trustworthy institutions, the churches rank on the bottom, lower even than political parties.

The drama of postmodern Germany is that many young people are blatantly incapable of developing community ties and understanding tradition as a means to mastering life. Instead, they want to forge their own identity, discard relationships and obligations, seek "freedom." In reality, they lose their identity because identity is always dependent on values and norms that give the individual his or her grounding. Without norms and values, individuals are left in a fickle state. Commitment is an alien concept. Narcissistically they revel in their self-reflection at the workplace or in the discotheque on Saturday nights.

Many people suffer from their inner emptiness, which explains the success of the esoteric movement and the psycho sects among the young. But young people, too, grow older, though TV commercials emit different signals: Stay young forever! Being old is taboo! However, the fact is that the question of life's meaning is being asked with ever-increasing urgency. And no amount of honky-tonk will ever squelch it. I am firmly convinced that in the long run no one is capable of living without commitments and moral guidelines.

The churches lost their monopoly on interpreting life and meaning a long time ago. But this cannot be the final word. I fervently believe in the doctrine of *ecclesia semper reformanda*—of the church's ability to always reform itself. Christ is by no means out of the picture. I am sure that in the future many people, perhaps individually, will seek His message and become disciples. Seen in this light, it may not be a bad thing that the churches vest themselves in the cloth of plurality, as long as their message remains unmistakable. The church must clearly distance itself from fads. Instead of groveling to the spirit of time, it must once again courageously proclaim Christ. Its task is to bring people to Jesus.

What does this mean for politics in the age of globalization? What type of politician do we need in postmodern times? Of course, a politician must know his stuff, refrain from lying to his people, and keep his feet firmly on the ground. That's what we have always expected of this profession. But like everybody else, a statesman needs models. Mine is Martin Luther. In 1521 he is supposed to have said during the Imperial Diet of Worms, "Here I stand. I cannot do otherwise. God help me, Amen!" Here is an example to follow—a man who publicly and courageously stood for his convictions and values.

The point of all this is that like our predecessors, perhaps even more so, postmodern men and women require a beacon to guide them through the chaos and confusion of our times, lest we never find our place—with dire consequences for every society. In my life, that beacon has been Christ. I have seen people follow other beacons—Hitler and Marx, for example. We all know the results. This is why I hope and pray that Bishop Dibelius's prediction will still come true, albeit belatedly.

This new century must be a century of the church—but of a church that stays faithful to its Lord instead of lusting after postmodernity's spurious spirits.

~~~~~

Dr. Hans Apel was West German Finance and Defense Minister. He now teaches economics at the University of Rostock and studies theology at the University of Hamburg.

ANTIDOTE
TO
MEDIA POSTMODERNITY

MARVIN OLASKY

Journalists are supposed to be up-to-the-minute and sometimes ahead of the minute, anticipating trends. So it should not be a surprise that some journalists as early as the 1920s were sounding very postmodern as they proclaimed that no reporter could convey an accurate view of reality. Henry Luce, founder of *Time* magazine, said, "Show me a man who thinks he's objective and I'll show you a man who's deceiving himself." Ivy Lee, a journalist who became known as the founder of public relations, said it was "humanly impossible" to state a fact: "All I can do is to give you my interpretation of the facts."

The Luce and Lee statements were part of the journalistic revolution that came early in the 1920s and 1930s as reporters, influenced by Marxism and Freudianism, redefined "objectivity." Marx had argued that much of what was called objectivity actually was class subjectivity, with one class-bound vision of the world placed against another, the-sis vs. antithesis. Freud contended that much of what affected individuals was unknown, even to the individuals themselves, so it could not be assumed that judgments were unimpaired.

Walter Lippmann, probably the most influential American newspaper columnist of the twentieth century, was a Marxist in his early years and an admirer of Freudian thought. He used those ideas to become in the 1920s a philosopher of journalism as well. Lippmann was sarcastic about reporters' claims to objectivity, arguing that "for the most part we do not see first, then define; we define first and then see."

The three L's—Lippmann, Luce, and Lee—had departed from the premodern American and European belief that truth was out there and journalists should seek it, gen-erally with wisdom gained from reading the Bible. They were pioneers in going beyond the modernist belief that whatever truth there was should be sought through human-ity's purported wisdom. Their assertion that there is no such thing as objective truth pointed to postmodernism.

Influenced by the three L's, journalists began to rede-fine the meaning of *objectivity* until it came to mean a bal-ancing of subjectivities, a recitation of several subjective views in a way that appeared evenhanded. As opposed to a standard dictionary definition of *objective*—"existing inde-pendent of mind; emphasizing or expressing the nature of reality as it is apart from subjective experience"—the out-come of the new "objectivity" might be neither truthful nor accurate, but who knew what accuracy, let alone truth, really was?

The Society of Professional Journalists concretized this in its code of ethics, proclaiming that "Truth is our ultimate goal," but "Objectivity in reporting the news is another goal, which serves as the hallmark of an experienced professional." Because objective truth did not exist, objectivity and truth were in two separate compartments: Quote person "x" and person "y" and you've done your job.

By the 1980s, however, journalists such as Linda Eller-bee were declaring bluntly that "there is no such thing as objectivity. Any reporter who tells you he's objective is lying to you." Full-fledged journalistic postmodernism—the belief that each reporter is a god unto himself, obliged not to report but to create his own reality—has developed least rapidly on local newspapers. A local reporter who tries to create his own reality runs into opposition when the story concerns something about which the reader has personal experience. A sports reporter, for example, cannot stray too far when describing a game witnessed by thousands or millions.

Journalistic postmodernism has reached its greatest development among feature writers with a descriptive flair or among those reporting from foreign climes that few readers comprehend. *New Yorker* writer Janet Malcolm has admitted fondly her readiness to treat real-life individuals essentially as fictional characters, ready to be depicted in a way that makes for drama, regardless of reality. The popular U.S. news show *60 Minutes* has become a ruthless example of this. Postmodernism gives journalists not only the freedom to construct whatever they choose, but a rationale for deconstruction. Knowledge, morality, and law are all social constructs, as are the truth claims that form the base of many of our institutions.

Journalists used to voice concern about increasing public cynicism in some areas, but now, because all establishments are seen to exist behind a façade of rationality, reporters have a responsibility to expose what is behind the façade. The thoroughly postmodern journalist has one response to virtually everything: "Bah, humbug."

There is an alternative: Although much is false, find out what is true, and stick with it. Gain journalistic freedom from cynicism by regaining a Christian understanding of the nature of human beings, the nature of God, and the nature of humanity's tasks and hopes. That biblical way is not based on confidence in humanity—people do naturally distort and lie—but on confidence in the objectivity of God. Just as a person assessing the strengths and weaknesses of his house is wise to consult the builder, so a person who wants to describe accurately the world God created should get information from its builder.

The biblical way is based on our ability, by God's grace, to study the Word, the Bible—God's objectivity—and apply it to everyday situations. Walter Cronkite once said that he was a liberal, which he then defined as one "not bound by doctrines or committed to a point of view in advance." But the biblical hope of arriving at accurate views is not to wipe our minds clean because then we are at the mercy of our limited vision. Instead, we should fill our minds with God's vision.

Biblical objectivity is the God's-eye view of things. Human beings cannot attain it, but on many subjects the message of Scripture is clear and we can come close enough to God's objectivity to know what is right to do and what is wrong. "Right" and "wrong" are not postmodern terms, but they will be around long after postmodernity has given way to an understanding that will be new because it is so old.

~~~~~

Dr. Marvin Olasky, a senior fellow of the Acton Institute for the Study of Religion and Liberty, is professor of journalism at the University of Texas at Austin and the editor of *World*, a biblically oriented newsweekly.

CHRIST VS. MANY GODS

GERALD R. MCDERMOTT

The most compelling question of the new millennium is which god to serve. Never before has there been such a cafeteria of religions from which to choose. Spirituality is no longer taboo, but in fact it is quite chic. The only problem is deciding which among the dizzying array of divinities to revere.

The postmodern answer to the problem is pluralism. By this is meant not the mere fact of many religions, but the philosophical conclusion that there is no right way to the divine, no final truth, no definitive knowledge of what is real. Therefore, one should think of many roads to salvation, indeed, many saviors.

Philosopher John Hick has articulated the best-known version of religious pluralism. With postmodernists generally, Hick insists that it is presumptuous to think of one true religion because we humans can never know Ultimate Reality without prejudice and distortion. Such postmodernist adherents claim that our understanding of the world outside of us is always colored and twisted by our particular experiences, which differ from everyone else's experiences. Therefore, when religions use precise and concrete language (such as Jesus' bodily resurrection or the existence of heavenly Buddhas), they are actually using humanly devised myths to sketch more abstract and imprecise realities.

Because we humans can never relate directly to Ultimate Reality and there is no real knowledge in faith, they aver, it does not really matter which religion we choose. Each religion points, with more or less equal indistinctness, to the only religious reality: the transformation of human existence from self-centeredness to Reality-centeredness. The problem with postmodern pluralism, however, is that it is anything but pluralist. It implicitly denounces all world religions as false in their particular beliefs (and, therefore, their billions of believers as deluded) and pronounces its own view of reality as the one true religion.

While rejecting any "God's-eye view" as impossible and all religions as partial, pluralism suggests that its own view transcends all others and is the only complete view available. Postmodern pluralism is as arrogant and intolerant as the fundamentalists who consign to hell all who disagree with them. It fails to affirm the validity of any religion that violates postmodern presuppositions, and it condescendingly suggests that non-postmoderns are saved by means only the postmodern knows.

Postmodernity celebrates universalism and condemns particularity, yet its gospel is a narrowly particular blend of late Western ideology: the ideas that individuality is the essence of the human being, technology is neutral, democracy is an absolute, and social Darwinism is a fact. Postmodern pluralism may be an appropriate religion for the marketplace, but it will never be accepted by the billions of devotees of the great world religions. It dismisses as irrelevant the very particulars of belief and practice, which believers in the world religions know to be the source of their power. Pluralism worships at the altar of moral disposition, which Buddhists and Muslims and Christians know is dead apart from (respectively) Dharma, Allah, and Jesus. Despite their own suspicion of the existing religions, postmoderns reject Christianity because, among other things, they think it shows contempt for all other religions.

But the Bible tells a different story. It shows the Old Testament God as wanting all the world to know Him. He said He would harden Pharaoh's heart so "the Egyptians will know that I am the LORD" (Exodus 14:4 NIV). The Bible hints at knowledge of God outside of Israel and the early Christian community. Even Jesus praised the faith of two "pagans"—a widow from Zarephath, notorious for its Baal-worship, and a Syrian general (Naaman), who worshiped a foreign god—and told the Jews in His hometown they should learn from them (Luke 4:24–29). The apostle Peter learned from Cornelius the Roman centurion, before Cornelius had heard the Gospel about Jesus, that "God does not show favoritism but accepts men from every nation who fear Him and do what is right" (Acts 10:34–35).

Postmoderns may be surprised to learn that historic but humble Christian faith affirms that other religions contain truth. Islam, for example, is true when it professes that God is one and greater than anything we can imagine. Jews speak truly when they confess that God is holy and demands conformity to His moral law. Pure Land Buddhists and *bhakti* Hindus teach truly when they explain that salvation comes not by human effort but by divine grace.

Christians can also say that other religions teach similar moral principles. They agree, for instance, with Confucius's Silver Rule: "Don't do anything you don't want done to you." They affirm the Buddha's precepts forbidding lying, stealing, murder, and sexual sin. They see the Bible's ethical teachings echoed in the Qur'an.

At the same time, however, Christians rightly say that Jesus Christ is unique. No other religious founder claimed to be God in the flesh (even Hindus concede their avatars only appear to be human). While the Buddha stated that he was no more than a man and said that we must be lamps unto ourselves, Jesus said that to see Him was to see God and that He is the light of the world.

Christianity's central claim, that Jesus rose from the dead, is remarkably well attested, though not "proven." Even secular historians admit that Jesus' disciples testified that they thrust their fingers into the holes in the body of the risen Christ and shared with Him a breakfast of fish and bread. Jesus also gives unique answers to the problem of pain. The Buddha taught his followers to escape suffering, whereas Jesus showed a way to conquer suffering by embracing it. This is why Buddhists look to a smiling Buddha seated on a lotus blossom while Christians worship a suffering Jesus nailed to a cross.

The *Tao Te Ching*, the bible of philosophical Taoists and many postmoderns, portrays Ultimate Reality as an Impersonal Something who requires resignation and accommodation to minimize, or perhaps escape, suffering. In contrast, the Scriptures proclaim that Ultimate Reality is a person who took up suffering into Himself. So the Christian God does not stand at a distance while we suffer; rather, He comes down and enters into our suffering with us. In fact, God Himself suffered the ultimate evil of death and overcame it, and He promises to take us up into that victory.

Muslims rightly believe that God is great. The Christian story of Jesus, however, reveals two kinds of greatness. One is illustrated by the emperor who sits high on his luxurious throne, far removed from the daily cares and pains of his subjects. He is surrounded by servants, who see that his will is obeyed throughout his kingdom. But there is also the greatness of a brilliant student who comes to the university and works hard to study medicine. After graduating, he does not set up a lucrative practice among the wealthy; instead, he goes among the country's poorest people to heal them. This is what God in Jesus Christ did. He revealed His greatness by stooping to save.

Finally, Jesus unveils an unparalleled intimacy with God. The Qur'an relates that God is closer to us than our jugular vein, but it never calls God "Father." Jesus, on the other hand, addressed God as "Daddy" (the best translation of the Aramaic *Abba*) and promised that He would draw believers up into that same intimacy.

In sum, Jesus Christ resolves the postmodern religious dilemma in ways that the other world religions do not: We no longer have to despair of our ability to find Ultimate Reality through reason and experience because final truth and love have broken into history in a person we can apprehend. Although this person does not denounce all that the other world religions offer, He promises to be their fulfillment.

~~~~

The Rev. Dr. Gerald McDermott, an Episcopal priest and prolific writer, teaches religion and philosophy at Roanoke College, Salem, Virginia.

FAITH AND MEDICINE RECONCILED

HAROLD G. KOENIG

Technological biomedicine has made tremendous strides during the twentieth century, improving the quality and length of life for millions of people. Despite this, there has been growing dissatisfaction among patients and health-care professionals over the mechanistic, impersonal, economically driven manner in which healthcare delivery sometimes occurs.

When people become ill, they want to be treated like whole persons, not simply as the kidney or heart in room 405 that needs to be fixed. For many, wholeness means body, mind, and spirit. Seasoned health professionals have long recognized the importance of psychological, social, and spiritual factors in the health and healing of their patients. Until recently, however, health professionals were reticent to address these issues, especially the subject of spirituality, because they lacked the time, lacked the training, or feared that this area was not in the domain of scientific medicine.

Such a perspective is rapidly changing in the postmodern world. One reason is that the doctor-patient relationship is changing from a paternalistic one (doctor knows best) to an egalitarian one (decisions made jointly by patient and doctor). People wish to have their spiritual or religious needs addressed and are becoming vocal about it, particularly when such beliefs and practices lie at the heart of how they cope with illness, how they give meaning to illness, and how they make decisions concerning medical care. Two-thirds of patients in a recent study indicated that their religious beliefs would affect the medical decisions they made when seriously ill.

Another reason for the change in practitioners' attitudes toward religion is the growing volume of research that is documenting connections between a person's religious involvement and health. While most of this research has been done in Christian populations, there is substantial evidence that Jewish, Muslim, and Eastern religious practices convey similar health benefits. The latter research, however, is dwarfed by the number of studies that examine the possible effects of traditional Judeo-Christian beliefs and practices on health and well-being. No fewer than 1,100 scientific studies have now explored these relationships, two-thirds or more showing that religious persons experience better mental health, better physical health, and need and use fewer expensive health services (see *The Handbook of Religion and Health*, Oxford University Press, 2000). According to some studies, active religious involvement may extend survival by as many as 7 to 14 years, equivalent to wearing a seat belt or not smoking cigarettes.

How religion actually accomplishes this is now under active investigation. First, a positive, optimistic belief system or worldview may affect the physical body by calming the nervous system and suppressing hormones such as cortisol and norepinephrine. Thereby, the immune system is boosted, and the cardiovascular function is stabilized. The extent of this "spirit-mind-body" interaction is only now beginning to be understood, but it is likely to be vast. Second, religious congregations provide emotional support. Social support buffers against emotional stress, improves disease detection, and encourages timely treatment. Third, religious doctrines discourage behaviors that adversely affect health (smoking, alcohol, risky sexual practices, etc.). Few other social institutions provide this combination of health-promoting resources.

In an amazing way, research at the turn of the millennium is discovering the exact opposite of what many health professionals since Sigmund Freud have thought about religion. The predominant view during the twentieth century was that religion, Christianity in particular, was either irrelevant to health or even had a negative influence. As healthcare professionals become aware of the volume and quality of research connecting religion and positive health, they are now wondering how to apply such findings to their clinical practices. Does this mean that patients ought to be encouraged to attend religious services, pray more, or read religious writings? Should religion or Christian beliefs be introduced by physicians to the nonreligious, adding this to a list of recommendations concerning diet, exercise, and smoking?

Probably not. None of this research shows that increasing religious activity or turning to Christ to improve health will result in better health. The utilitarian use of religion as a means to some other end (called "extrinsic" religiosity) is not associated with better health. Instead, health may simply be a byproduct of a devout faith that is pursued for the right reasons.

More sensible and sensitive application of these new and exciting findings, however, is possible. Many patients already use religious beliefs and practices to help them cope with the stress of medical illness; this has been particularly true in studies of Christians. Information about the patients' religious beliefs and the amount of support they receive from their religious community often has direct relevance for patient care. Healthcare professionals might inquire about religious practices and find out how patients use them to cope and how this influences their medical decisions. Appropriate referrals to chaplains or clergy could be made when spiritual needs arise. Both nursing schools and medical schools are beginning to train healthcare professionals to take a patient's spiritual history, just as they might inquire about the patient's living circumstances and social environment.

More than 70 of 126 U.S. medical schools now have courses on religion, spirituality, and medicine, a dramatic change from less than a decade ago when only a handful of schools had such courses. As a result, patients in this postmodern era may soon find their physicians and other health professionals asking about and supporting their religious beliefs and practices, particularly those that do not directly conflict with medical care.

Such inquiries should be "patient centered." In other words, the focus will be on supporting what the patient finds helpful and familiar, not on introducing or imposing new religious beliefs or practices. Some healthcare professionals may also be willing to pray with patients, particularly if the patient requests this. Most patients greatly appreciate when healthcare providers are sensitive to and support the religious or spiritual beliefs that matter so much to them, particularly at a time when they are struggling to find meaning and purpose in lives threatened by change. Respect for those without such beliefs is also essential.

In the twenty-first century, we will likely see more healthcare systems linking with religious communities. The number of older adults is increasing as Baby Boomers age. The cost of healthcare is rising. The resources to provide that care are limited, and there is a backlog of people who are unable to enter nursing homes or acute care hospitals and who thus need care in the community. This will force the trend to link healthcare and faith communities. In many cases a parish or congregational nurse will facilitate this relationship. A parish nurse is a registered nurse, often a member of the religious community, who educates church volunteers, screens members for health problems, and provides support for sick members of the congregation and their families.

By mobilizing volunteers from the congregation and providing support in the home, the parish nurse helps to keep the sick person out of the hospital, thus avoiding expensive institutional care. Studies are beginning to show that religious volunteers who live out their faith by helping others end up having better mental health, greater purpose in life, and even greater longevity—a win-win situation for everyone.

The research linking religious activity (especially volunteering) with better mental and physical health will presumably end one of modernity's peculiar legacies: The high wall of separation between religion and medicine that was erected during the nineteenth and twentieth centuries appears to be coming down.

~~~~~

Harold G. Koenig, M.D., is associate professor of psychiatry and medicine at Duke University Medical Center and editor in chief of *Research News & Opportunities in Science and Theology*.

PREACHING
TO POSTMODERNS

JAY C. ROCHELLE

Phillips Brooks, a nineteenth-century Episcopal priest and bishop in Boston, said that preaching was "the communication of truth through personality." Three assumptions lie buried in this simple statement. First, truth is there and it is available. With this assertion, I am sure that Bishop Brooks thought of the Christian Scripture as the source of that truth. Second, truth may be communicated between and among people. Third, truth may be communicated through personality because God became flesh and dwelt among us, thus authorizing the transmission of spiritual truth through personal means.

Today all three of these assumptions are challenged. Brooks may be surprised that people think of preaching as the communication of *opinion* through personality. That's the postmodern understanding: We live in such a radically pluralistic period that no one can claim a corner on the truth. At best we can share our opinions or perceptions of how the world works. Preaching is audacious. To use rhetoric to convince a person of the truth of a perception is tricky business. People think of preaching as if it were advertising on radio or TV. You mute it unless you happen to have a yen for the product. So it is with Christian preaching. You avoid it unless you have a yen for the product.

What do preachers think they are up to? Here again we walk on difficult ground for postmoderns. Preachers think a particular text makes truth available. That's what people mean by the "inspiration" of the Bible. It's a way to say that we think that in this book God reveals truth to us. The operative word is "reveals"—as if God were both hidden and important. Christian preachers think this book was ultimately written because God is revealed in a particular person, Jesus of Nazareth. God, the eternal and indefinable mystery, entered the realm of contingency, relativity, and definition.

No wonder we're in trouble. The whole idea is "impossible" and has been since the beginning. No amount of logic can prove it. So what makes this postmodern century different from any previous one? After all, people have talked about "the scandal of particularity" since the beginning: That God should take up residence in one solitary Jew is an offense to religious sensibilities.

The belief that the contingencies of history cannot bear eternal truth has been around longer than Gotthold Lessing, who put words to it in the eighteenth century. So what's new? In earlier centuries a framework permitted the Gospel to be preached and, occasionally, to flourish. You can call that framework Christendom, as do historians, or you can call it Meta-narrative, as do Jean-Francois Lyotard and postmodern critics. An agreed upon set of understandings about how reality is best approached held majority position in society, sometimes by force. The Inquisition is the textbook example of trying to force people to accept a big picture against their personal judgment.

There is no big picture. This realization meets with mixed responses. Some will say "What a shame" and wring their hands in nostalgia. On the other side, one hears rejoicing: "It's about time!" No more Inquisitions. Unfortunately for rejoicing postmoderns, humans seem to have a drive to sum up reality in a package. We look for the big picture, despite current disclaimers. We are not satisfied with shards; we want to glue them together to make a pot.

Wallace Stevens wrote for most of us when the strings of lights that subdivided the waters in the harbor at Key West told him of the "blessed rage for order" that gives birth to metaphysics. We find it hard to say anything that could not lead beyond description to a level where we connect the dots in coherent sense. Metaphysical yearnings are built in; they come with the package of humanity and language. Here, perhaps, is a clue to the place of preaching in postmodernity.

A number of searches keep preaching open. Aesthetics, ethics, and pragmatism are three. Some people look for beauty and some for goodness. The postmodern gang tells us that most do not seek truth these days. These Aristotelian companions to truth may be a draw, however. Beautiful liturgy is attractive. Icons may be one reason for the rising attraction of Orthodoxy to young people. Frederica Mathewes-Green, an Orthodox Christian and popular writer, says people show up for the exotic beauty of Orthodox liturgy for a month. Then they hear the liturgy confront them with the Gospel; at this point, many leave, though some stay. Aesthetic needs are powerful and draw people to a sphere where Christ is heard in art and music.

Goodness is a draw. Preaching, however, is not about goodness. It is about Law and Gospel. Preaching about goodness is boring or offensive for the wrong reasons. Nobody wants to be told how to live. At most you may suggest paths of behavior, not ordain them. People seek the reason why they live. According to legend, Cary Grant came to visit W. C. Fields on his deathbed. Fields, a known atheist, was reading a Bible, and Grant caught him in the act. When Grant asked why he was reading the Scriptures, Fields said, "I'm just looking for the loopholes." We can identify with his wry humor.

People show up at church because "it works for me," as the jargon goes. That's what pragmatism means: It works. Something in the proclamation of the Gospel makes sense of your world. The search for what works has led many people through the doors of church. If something is revealed that makes sense of their lives, they stay. This is why the intellectual rigor that informs good preaching cannot be replaced by sentimentalism or, worse, the appeal to feeling that occupies much that passes for Christianity these days.

Sense and sentiment are not the same. People deserve more than fleeting feelings. They deserve solid content and intellectual depth, both of which bear silent witness that the Gospel is worthy of our attention. What brings folks, I suspect, is a combination of these searches. Even in these postmodern times, however, what will keep them coming is that they discover shreds of truth in the proclamation. There is a yearning to find a truth worth living. I hasten to add that proclamation may be both audible and visible. Sacraments and icons preach by their very existence. Postmodernity may bring the institution under severe question, but the Gospel arises wherever Word and Sacrament may be found.

We try to make sense of our world. To do this we need a framework to interpret what comes onto our perceptual screen. Metaphysics comes in through the back door when we have swept it out the front. We cannot help this drive. Gospel may be spoken and shown to this search, this blessed rage for order. A well-known unbeliever kept showing up at worship led by C. H. Spurgeon, the famed nineteenth-century English preacher. When asked why he attended though he didn't believe the message, the unbeliever replied, "True, but he [Spurgeon] does." There is a place for making a witness to the Gospel, for offering it as a way to see the world in this postmodern parenthesis.

Preachers of the Gospel believe they are witnessing to truth. Otherwise who would engage in this act? They base this claim on faithfulness to the Bible they preach, or they may base it on their experience of Christ. As long as preachers remain faithful, people may come with the words, "I don't believe this, but he does." The apostle Paul, no slouch at this preaching business, said faith comes through hearing (Romans 10:17) when the content of what's preached is Christ.

~~~~~

The Rev. Dr. Jay Cooper Rochelle, a former seminary professor, is pastor emeritus of St. Timothy's Lutheran Church, Allentown, Pennsylvania.

ASHES
ON POSTMODERN HEADS

MARK NOLL

In a postmodern world, people are supposedly defining their own truths, doing their own thing. In a postmodern scheme, we create truth, we do not simply receive what has been given to us. Yet on Ash Wednesday, hundreds of millions of people around the world will do pretty much the same thing for pretty much the same reason. And they will do it because previous generations have passed this rite down to them. As they do it, they will be suggesting that truth can endure across the centuries.

In the Western Christian calendar, Ash Wednesday is the beginning of Lent. Ash Wednesday and Lent are observed more consistently among Catholics than among Protestants, but in recent years an increasing number of the latter have also been marking the day and the season. For Christians, these special times in the calendar call upon humans to change what they do because of what God in Christ has done for them.

Lent points toward the great events of the Passion Week—the betrayal, the trial, the persecution, the crucifixion, the death, and then the resurrection of Jesus Christ. Lent asks for special concentration of mind and even real changes in behavior as a way to prepare for the commemoration of these climactic events. Because of what happened nearly 2,000 years ago, Christians believe they are to be different—and to live differently—today.

Ash Wednesday and Lent came into existence to encourage such responses to Christ's Passion. More than one thousand years ago, the church began to set aside the weeks before Easter as a special time of repentance. It may even have been in the first Christian centuries that these observances began. A common practice in this special season was to read selected texts from the Hebrew Scriptures, which Christians call the Old Testament. One such passage was taken from Isaiah, "Is not this the fast that I choose: to loose the bonds of injustice, to undo the thongs of the yoke, to let the oppressed go free . . .?" (Isaiah 58:6 NRSV).

Originally, however, Lent was not for everyone. Instead, it was designed for people who had committed extraordinary public sins and had been excommunicated, that is, formally dismissed from the fellowship of believers. Ash Wednesday was the day when these excommunicated ones could be brought back into the church. It began a season of worship services during which the excommunicated performed special acts of penitence, including dressing in sackcloth (a kind of burlap) and covering themselves with ashes to show their sorrow for their sins. The other believers fasted and prayed for these excommunicated ones.

All this activity pointed toward the actual restoration of these repentant Christians who had been excommunicated. Sometime during Lent there would be a special service of reconciliation during which those who had been excommunicated were readmitted to the fellowship. The leaders of worship would lay hands on their excommunicated brethren. They would be prayed for, then they would once again join fellow believers in celebrating the Lord's Supper.

Such services of public repentance could have a great effect. So impressive, in fact, were these services that the pressure grew to let all the faithful share in such an experience. The ashes that had been preserved for excommunicated public sinners were now given to all. It was clear that ordinary sins and ordinary rebellion against God needed repentance and the restoration of faith too. Thus was born the season of Lent as a time of special reflection on the need of all to repent, to turn from evil, and to take refuge in Christ.

Ash Wednesday was the day to inaugurate this special season. Special prayers and readings were said as the faithful came to be marked on the forehead with ashes in the sign of a cross. Most readings and prayers were a variation on "Dust thou art, and to dust shalt thou return" (Genesis 3:29 KJV). But why, in this age of self-affirmation, fret over repentance for sins? How can such an ancient ceremony still make sense in a postmodern world? What is the point of it all? The Christian response about the need for repentance is quite clear. Unless we acknowledge our sin before God, believers testify, we cannot enjoy God.

Richard John Neuhaus has written a moving book of meditations on the seven last words from the cross in which he takes up these questions. As Neuhaus puts it, "To belittle our sins is to belittle ourselves, to belittle who it is that God creates and calls us to be. To belittle our sins is to belittle their forgiveness, to belittle the love of the Father who welcomes us home."

We repent, so the church says, because unless we acknowledge our sin, we cannot know the one who rescues from sin. We repent because unless we acknowledge our sin, we cannot know the Savior. As for carrying ancient rituals into a postmodern era, Ash Wednesday and Lent may be as relevant now as ever. A fascination with power and its abuses characterizes almost all postmodern thinking.

To these concerns, the cross of Christ should be a marvel. It presents abject powerlessness of the kind that so infuriated Nietzsche and is such a puzzle to the sociobiologists as a positive good. The cross wins people over not by taking but by giving. At the end of the day, the cross is not a symbol of postmodernity, but what it stands for, as affirmation through loss, should speak to the postmodern condition.

Postmodernists are also keen on the tremendous differences that divide human beings. Again, while not able to go the full distance with most versions of postmodernism, Christians can point to the cross as an affirmation of astounding human diversity. The human race has demonstrated an all but infinite creativity in its sins, yet all are welcome—all may stand together even with the fullest differences possible—at the foot of the cross.

The point of Ash Wednesday and of the Lenten season that follows is to change us as we contemplate the cross. The little sign that is made with the ashes speaks for an immense reality. As the apostle Paul put it in the letter to the Galatians, the cross reveals an unbelievable truth: "The Son of God . . . loved me and gave Himself for me" (2:20 NIV). It is the cross of Christ that calls for repentance and makes possible repentance. Christ's death on the cross means that we may have spiritual life. Because He suffered for sin that He did not commit, we are freed from the sins that we commit every day. So it is that the cross, a symbol of vile suffering, can become for the Christian an occasion of joy.

The English poet George Herbert put this mysterious truth as well as it could be put. In writing about motives for praising God, he considered that the lute is made of wood, the same substance of which the cross was constructed. To Herbert that was an apt conjunction indeed:

Awake, my lute, and struggle for thy part
With all thy art.
The cross taught all wood to resound his name
Who bore the same.
His stretched sinews taught all strings, what key
Is best to celebrate this most high day.

For Christian believers, Ash Wednesday is a sober day. It inaugurates a season of self-denial. But the message, above all, is of faith and hope and love.

~~~~~

Dr. Mark Noll teaches history at Wheaton College, Wheaton, Illinois.

RISKY BUSINESS

HOWARD A. DAHL

Postmodernity is not the most common topic in board-rooms or at business seminars. Blank stares would probably meet anybody who would bring it up. But from a Christian perspective, postmodernity is a matter that must be discussed in the business world. Christians are particularly well placed to make others aware of the extent to which postmodernism affects the life of every one of us, business-people included.

In many contemporary Christian circles, one can hear a blanket indictment of postmodernity. This reaction reminds us of how Communism was condemned in the 1950s and 1960s and secular humanism in the 1970s and 1980s. For many, postmodernity is today's repository of evil. But this is not altogether fair; postmodernity is too multi-faceted to be dismissed simply with a few derisive remarks.

In his great book *Democracy in America,* Alexis de Tocqueville said that in no civilized country has less attention been paid to philosophy than in the United States. However, back in 1840 he foresaw two philosophical and societal developments that would occur more than 150 years later:

1. Pragmatism. De Tocqueville did not use this term, but he contrasted the Americans' dislike for theory with their strong bent toward the practical. John Dewey later developed pragmatism into the only original philosophical system of this country. Postmodernity perverted it into the self-centered attitude of "everything goes." I shall return to this later.

2. Pluralism, multiculturalism, and globalism. De Tocqueville wrote, "Our means of intellectual intercourse united the remotest parts of the earth; and men cannot remain strangers to each other, or be ignorant of what is taking place in any corner of the globe."

Thus de Tocqueville anticipated a reality we businesspeople face everywhere and every day. It is not an altogether negative postmodern reality because the postmodernists do show concern for people outside their own reference group. They call them "other." Every day, the "other" confronts businesspeople via e-mail, the Internet, and travel. International commerce has brought people of different cultural, religious, and ethnic backgrounds together.

This presents a challenge to Christian businesspeople. How are we to see the "other"? The answer surely lies in Scripture. The "other" is a postmodern variant of the alien, the stranger, or even the Good Samaritan, whose postmodern manifestation the Christian businessperson should be. But this is where the parallels between postmodernity and Christian business attitudes end. Like modernity's intellectual luminaries, such as Marx, Freud or Nietzsche, postmodernity's thinkers are often hostile to God and honest commerce as well. Like yesterday's intellectuals, their contemporary successors show contempt for the kind of moral pragmatism that must define a responsible Christian businessperson. Postmodern pragmatism is amoral.

The leading American voice of postmodernism is the philosopher Richard Rorty. He sees himself as a radical pragmatist in the tradition of John Dewey, whom he describes as "a postmodernist before his time." Like the Marxist intellectuals of the past, Rorty is antagonistic to business, and he denies God. Yet it would be simplistic for Christians to dismiss him because Rorty holds some postmodern views that Christians could affirm, chiefly his concern for the "other." Rorty, who identifies himself as a "freeloading atheist," buys in to the traditional Judeo-Christian perspective that the stranger deserves to be treated with dignity, especially if that stranger has previously been stripped of that dignity. That's a good start, though Christians must go a step further. They must "love their enemies" and be "kind to the wicked and the ungrateful." It is a great weakness of postmodernism that it does not provide a sound foundation for treating "others" this way. Its variant of pragmatism precludes such treatment because it is ultimately self-centered.

Then again, Christians can follow a statement by Rorty that acknowledges a great tension in affirming postmodern beliefs, namely, that postmodernism is really relativism, which is self-refuting. Can we be good without God? Rorty arrives at a devastating conclusion about the concept of being open-minded to all ideas: One can "become so open-minded that our brains [fall] out."

The business world is not immune to the kind of relativism Rorty discusses. For some time now I have been making it a point to ask acquaintances, "Do you have an example of making a decision because it was the right thing to do, even though it cost you a lot of money?" I was amazed by how many people could not come up with an answer because this question is not even on their screen. The expedient mind does not ask: What's right? It asks: What works? This means that "right and wrong" are no longer generally accepted categories. Therefore, Christians must part company with postmodernity's form of pragmatism at this point.

Committed Christians do not have the relativistic option of expediency. They know that God has called them to their position, whatever it might be. Hence, they cannot be satisfied with what suits them at any given moment; instead, they must ask: What is the right thing to do? We Christians must view life beyond the scope of modernity, postmodernity, or any other temporal whim. For us no alternative exists to Christ, the incarnate truth of God who made Himself small for us. It is for us that Christ died, as we remember especially in this season of Lent. Because of His resurrection, we have eternal life.

This truth calls us to discipleship in faith, and doing the right thing for the love of our neighbor is a fruit of that faith. Being human, we are prone to err time and again. But as Christians we also know that we can repent and receive forgiveness and renewal from Christ. The knowledge of this truth makes it impossible for any Christian, including a Christian in business, to indulge in postmodernity's relativist profusion of "truths."

In the parlance of commerce, postmodernity is simply too risky a business.

~~~~

Howard Dahl manufactures farm equipment in Fargo, North Dakota.

TEACHING GOD'S WRATH

DAVID WHITFORD

W hat the Nazis did to the Jews would be wrong if they did it here; but I really can't say that it was wrong for them to do it there. They had their own culture they were trying to protect." I used to think statements like that were the creations of over-the-top columnists or academics with an agenda. No longer! I now have two years of teaching Introduction to Ethics under my belt. College students really do have a hard time condemning the Nazis. It's not even their fault, sadly. They've been taught and fed a steady diet of postmodernism's only absolute: Truth is situational and relative. My students, and those like them around the country, are simply demonstrating that they really did learn something in high school.

Does the church—does Christ—have anything to say to a college student who can't condemn the Nazis? I think it does, but to do so will require recapturing a long forgotten attribute of God: wrath. Just the word sounds strangely incongruent when thinking about God. We've been taught and told that God is love. While this is undoubtedly true, there is much to be learned from a reinvigorated under-standing of God's anger.

Simply put, without wrath there is no judgment. With-out judgment there is no hope. Wrath became an unpopular attribute of God somewhere in the nineteenth century, when G. F. W. Hegel and Friedrich Schleiermacher (in dif-ferent ways) both attempted to keep Christianity relevant to the emerging "scientific/modern" mind-set. For the sake of relevance, however, they sacrificed integrity. It was argued that God could not be both loving and wrathful at the same time. Today, we continue to operate largely under the same presupposition.

As a second-year seminarian serving a large suburban Philadelphia congregation as an intern, I was asked to preach at one of the noontime Holy Week services. The Scripture lesson for the day was Jesus' cleansing of the temple. I had given the lesson to the church secretary and had prepared to preach on it. When I arrived, however, a new lesson was in its place. My sermon title was gone, and I was asked politely to choose something else.

The pastor read an innocuous lesson. Brashness being a gift of the young, I stood up and preached my original ser-mon anyway. It was on wrath and anger. I preached that ser-mon because I believed then, and believe still, that we have much to learn from God's anger. Contrary to popular opin-ion, wrath and judgment are integral to any profound love. The cliché that the antithesis of love is not anger but indif-ference is correct in this regard.

God is not indifferent. God is loving, and that love sometimes demands righteous anger. Righteous anger is, indeed, a necessary attribute of God, an attribute worthy of emulation. The story of Jesus in the temple is important. In fact, it is so important that all four evangelists record the event. It is important because it runs contrary to the meek and mild image of Jesus we are usually fed. It is important because it reminds us that God does get angry. Jesus got angry when He saw the temple turned into a flea market.

God always gets angry when we turn gifts into perversion. When human beings turn love into lust, when we turn a living into an obsession, when we turn churches into country clubs, God gets angry. God's righteous anger judges the powerful when they abuse the weak. When those with money hoard and turn a gift into greed, God is not indifferent. What does Jesus have to say to postmodernity's fascination with relativity? Simply, He says there are limits and there are things worthy of our anger. God wants us to use and appreciate (even be thankful for) His gifts.

God wants us to enjoy one another in fellowship. But when this gift is turned on its head and perverted into ways to take advantage of others, God does become angry—at sin. The Gospel proclaims that Christ paid the price for human sinfulness and that God's mercy covers our postmodern indifference to wrongdoing. But God's righteous anger remains: at injustice, at egregious mistreatment, at our inhumanity toward others. As human beings we ought to emulate that aspect of God's relationship to us among ourselves. God's anger is not rage, and it is not rash. It is righteous, and it is purposeful. It is not abusive, but it does set limits.

Righteous anger is something my college students still need to experience. If you are a parent and your child is doing drugs, that is a time to be angry. Not the type of anger that screams and hits, but the type of burning anger that will make sure that rules are set and obeyed, that help is sought, and that drug abuse is overcome. Righteous anger can teach us much today. It can remind us that because God has created all people, they are worthy of just and humane treatment. It can remind us that some things, no matter when and no matter where, are wrong and must be resisted.

What the Nazis did to the Jews would be wrong in this society, but it would also be wrong anywhere. Postmodernity still needs to learn that lesson.

~~~~

The Rev. Dr. David Whitford teaches religion and philosophy at Claflin University, Orangeburg, South Carolina.

GOING BOLDLY
WITH THE NET

DAVID DAVENPORT

When El Nino ravaged the California coast several winters ago, some described the massive storms as a "500-year rain." Likewise, our society is experiencing a 500-year set of changes. Not only are we witnessing an economic shift from the industrial era to the information age, but we are experiencing a corresponding cultural shift from the modern age to postmodernity. Every institution, including the church, must adapt in fundamental ways to these changes.

Christianity is not alone in resisting change. Most of us sympathize with the 97-year-old man who reacted to an interviewer's observation that, over his lifetime, he had seen a lot of changes. "Yes," the man responded, "and I was opposed to every one of them." After learning to speak its message to the modern mind, the church is often reluctant to adapt the timeless message of Christianity to the new postmodern culture. Rather than bemoaning or opposing the cultural shift to postmodernity, the church should be looking for new opportunities and dangers. After all, no worldly culture is truly Christian, and the modern era, with its emphasis on the power of science and rationalism, was hardly an ally to faith in God.

Postmodernism rejects the modern idea that society is driven by science and rationalism toward a better way of thinking and living. Instead, the postmodern view is that we live among a diverse and equally valid set of philosophies, cultures, and worldviews. The first opportunity, then, for Christians in a postmodern world is to take their seat at the table along with other philosophies and worldviews. Long denied a seat at the table of modern science and rationalism, Christianity can take its place at least among the diversity of spiritual and other worldviews now celebrated by postmoderns. As theologian Robert Nash Jr. observed, people are thirsting after something that will bring meaning to life because science and reason haven't provided the answers. Christians should no longer accept second-class citizenship in the academy or elsewhere, and they should begin connecting with a culture that is more open to spiritual things.

A second opportunity for Christians in a postmodern world is to help people make good choices. Another key characteristic of postmodernity is the myriad of choices. The modern world had three television channels; the postmodern cable or dish has hundreds. The modern ice-cream store offered a handful of flavors; today there are dozens. Similarly, we live in a time when information is doubling every year, and lifestyles of all kinds proliferate. Amid all these choices, people are seeking a compass, a set of navigational aids. When St. Paul speaks of a more excellent way, when Jesus says He is the way, we speak language that reaches postmodern needs. Churches should offer classes and materials, especially for young people, that help them navigate in a world of choices.

Becoming even more specific, young people in the postmodern world are highly interested in family. Believing that their modern parents caused them great pain in fractured families, surveys indicate that being good parents and having strong families is a high priority among postmodern youth. What a rich opportunity for the church to minister and provide resources for the family!

Similarly, it is clear that the postmodern world is multicultural and global in shape. Here again is an opportunity for Christians to work in the postmodern world to make the church truly global. Mission efforts, international opportunities, and intercultural programs have unusual promise in this era.

I recall one of our children coming home from high school one day and saying, "Why is it okay to be anything at my school but a Christian?" Although the highest values of postmodernism are relativism and tolerance, that acceptance does not always extend to a worldview, such as Christianity, that teaches absolute truth. Here, I believe, the church will have to introduce people to Jesus and His story and connect people to the power of the Gospel and the Holy Spirit. My sense is that the "four spiritual laws" or the "five steps to salvation" were wise approaches to the modern mind but not to the postmodern man or woman. Perhaps only in hearing Jesus' story will postmodern thinkers come to consider His values and realize that some values are higher than others.

Another challenge is low denominational loyalty among postmoderns. Indeed, postmoderns tend to integrate and not debate. They are as likely to look at world philosophies and religions as they are other Christian churches. It may take greater collaboration among Christians if we are to present God effectively to the postmodern world.

May I suggest that one ally the church generally overlooks at present is technology? Although the Internet is widely described as the most powerful communication tool yet created, and we Christians have the most powerful message ever communicated, we are not using technology as we could to reach the postmodern world. The first word of the Great Commission is "go," and the Internet gives us an opportunity to "go" into all the world and reach every postmodern creature. We must not be reluctant to use postmodern methods to carry the timeless message of Christ!

If you have seen the musical *Les Misérables*, you will remember the dramatic scene at the barricades during the French Revolution. Young people were crossing the barricades to a new world, often facing grave dangers and loss in the process. This is how I picture our mission as Christians in a postmodern world. We stand at the barricades of change, helping postmoderns find their way in a new world within the context of faith in Christ.

The same God of the premodern and modern worlds is the God of the postmodern world as well. It is our mission and calling to stand at the barricades of change and be certain that His message is proclaimed in these new times.

~~~~

The Rev. Dr. David Davenport, a minister, lawyer, former president of Pepperdine University, and CEO of Christianity.com, is a senior fellow at the Hoover Institution at Stanford University.

No Better Time
for Mission

Robert E. Reccord

Charles Dickens captured the attention of the literary world when he began *A Tale of Two Cities* with "It was the best of times. It was the worst of times." The power of the paradox has always drawn attention as the power of the magnet draws iron filings. And paradox well describes the culture in which we find ourselves.

As I write this, it is the best of times: Unemployment is relatively low; there are more millionaires than at anytime in our history; medical science is monthly bringing new answers to our health problems as society ages; more than 360,000 churches dot the U.S. landscape. But it is also the worst of times: Kids are killing kids; abortion has taken millions of lives; sexual activity among young people remains high; public education struggles to meet even the most basic goals; terrorism threatens our nation and the world as never before. The Bible and prayer have been ushered out of our schools so no one will be offended. Often those in the church are as caught up in the negative trends as the rest of society.

Much of this cultural paradox traces its roots to society's philosophical shift from a modernist view of life to a postmodern outlook. The Renaissance period (1300–1600) gave birth to the modernist idea that truth could only be discovered through reason as opposed to divine revelation. This philosophy saw human beings as primarily rational and only negligibly spiritual. Modernism answered the question "What is truth?" with empirical scientific methods and analytical processes. Any truth that couldn't be rationally observed and quantified through rational empiricism could not be trusted. Modernists viewed the supernatural as an unnatural part of life.

But at some point in the 1960s, society began to shift. Suddenly, truth no longer exists in the objective case, even within rationalism. Instead, each culture or individual determines truth for itself; no truth is absolute for all people, in all places, at all times. Instead, truth has become subjectively grounded in one's experience rather than in God's revelation or even in scientific evidence. As a result, every religion or faith is equally valid because truth is determined by a person's experience. Just as the Declaration of Independence states that all men are created equal, this postmodern view asserts that all claims to truth must also be equal.

Into that vacuum stepped syncretistic writers such as Deepak Chopra, who proclaims that our understanding of God should be as encompassing as human experience and that God's "royalty" is integrated into our perceptions.

How does all this impact the way contemporary Christians take the Gospel of Christ to the world—and especially Western civilization? It might surprise many to discover that our postmodern age shares more similarities with the first century, in which Jesus launched the mission of the New Testament church, than with any other time since. Family breakdown, syncretism and religion, relativism and values, multiculturalism, disenchantment with institutions, and swelling individualism formed the backdrop against which the mission of the New Testament church moved forth. It is the same backdrop today.

Other postmodern characteristics are common to every generation. Human beings have always tried to define God and salvation on their own terms. Every generation has rebelled against absolutes. But truth has a way of catching up with us, and it leaves those who try to defy it with fractured bodies, broken relationships, empty souls, or lives devoid of meaning and purpose.

But God does not depend upon us or upon the trends of our times when it comes to establishing a relationship with Himself. He doesn't wait for us to search after Him. He seeks us. In Luke 19:10, Jesus proclaimed, "The Son of Man came to seek and to save the lost!" (RSV). In three of His best-known parables—The Lost Sheep, The Lost Coin, The Lost Son (Luke 15)—Jesus reiterated His life's mission statement of seeking once again those who are lost.

Christianity is not muted or impotent in this environment. The Gospel shines even brighter against the darkness and confusion created by humankind's quest for a self-styled utopia. Maybe that explains why the ministry I am observing among Southern Baptists, whom I serve, is exploding. This year more than 20,000 junior and senior high students will volunteer to spend a week of their summer in the inner city, rebuilding substandard houses for the poor while actively sharing their faith. Some 24,000 volunteers served 1.8 million hot meals at 151 disaster venues in 1999 and 2000. A total of 5,000 full-time mission personnel serve across North America with another 5,000 overseas, and the numbers are growing at record rates in both arenas. College students are volunteering to spend between one and four semesters somewhere in North America in mission ministries during their undergraduate years, a growth rate of 65 percent last year alone. And approximately 180,000 volunteers gave their time to short-term mission projects throughout North America last year.

Why is this happening? Because committed Christians understand that the philosophy of postmodernism doesn't fulfill the emptiness of the human soul. Many of those participating are themselves refugees of this failed approach. The apostle Paul wrote, "Where sin increased, grace abounded all the more" (Romans 5:20b RSV). In a world of no absolutes, Christ's unwavering claims stand tall. The freedom He offers is a refuge to those tossed about in our day of moral contradiction and philosophical chaos. In a society that values personal experience above all else, individual accounts of lives radically changed by Christ carry more weight than ever.

Teresa grew up in a home in which her parents constructed a view of God based not on Scripture, but on their own preferences. She was taught that there are no absolutes. All lifestyles and beliefs were seen as equal. As a result, her biography reads more like a rap sheet:

Age 6: She was molested by a trusted family friend.

Age 7: She began stealing from her mother's purse regularly.

Age 10: She started smoking.

Age 12: She had her first sexual experience.

Age 14: She became sexually active regularly.

Age 15: She became an alcoholic.

Age 17: She delved into drugs and was gang-raped.

Age 18: She became involved in prostitution.

Age 26: She tried lesbianism and worked at the Edgar Cayce (New Age) Association for Research and Enlightenment.

At age 31, Teresa came face-to-face with the seeking Christ and found that He alone could fill the vacuum left in her postmodern world. Truth became absolute and real in

Jesus Christ. Her private world, which she had seen personally disintegrate, took a radical turn with this new commitment. Her hardened countenance softened, a new job provided a new lease on life, and she became a volunteer through her new church home, reaching out to others trapped in a postmodern world.

As long as God stays in the "business" of turning lives around (and He always will), there will be Christians who are actively taking the message of salvation to those around them, no matter what the cultural and philosophical trends of the time. As the apostle Paul wrote to the early church, "We are ambassadors for Christ, since God is making His appeal through us . . ." (2 Corinthians 5:20 NRSV).

Amid the postmodern world's "worst of times," people such as Teresa are discovering they can still have "the best of times" through new life in Christ.

~~~~~

The Rev. Dr. Robert E. Reccord is president of the Southern Baptist Convention's North American Mission Board.

No Ground
under Our Feet

Uwe Siemon-Netto

In the prologue to *Letters and Papers from Prison*, Dietrich Bonhoeffer made a prophetic observation, one that read like a description of the postmodern state of affairs: "One may ask whether there have ever before in human history been people with so little ground under their feet—people to whom every available alternative seemed equally intolerable, repugnant and futile."

The point has been made before that the Nazi regime, which ultimately hanged this German theologian, was a precursor of postmodern times. Adolf Hitler substituted the transcendent truth of premodern society with his own flexible "truths." In the absence of divinity, there were no absolutes either.

Like the Communists and other atheistic totalitarians, the Nazis felt free to raise or lower their level of morality at their whim. The results were twofold: Millions died, and the others were left with a sense of futility. They felt no ground under their feet.

How does such a lack of absolutes affect society? Consider Dresden, once Germany's most beautiful city, which became part of Communist East Germany, a collectivized society that was so blatantly untrue that people managed to retain their sanity only by leading two separate lives simultaneously. One was the "official" life, in which nobody dared to speak his mind or act as she really wished. Then there was the other life in what Eastern Europeans used to call "niches"—virtual spaces where one could act, talk, love, laugh, and enjoy oneself normally in the company of like-minded friends.

Often church groups acted as "niches" until they were able to play a pivotal role in imploding the untruthful political system. But when this system vanished, Western-style postmodernity filled the void, eradicating most of the niches. This caused a severe form of a condition the French sociologist Emile Durkheim introduced toward the end of the nineteenth century. He called it anomie.

As a sociological category, anomie is characterized by instability, the breakdown of social norms, institutional disorganization, and the divorce between socially valid goals and the means to achieve them. People living under these conditions experience a psychological disorder: rootlessness, futility, anxiety, and amorality.

The anomie sensed by as farsighted a man as Bonhoeffer, who lived in a totalitarian system, has now afflicted citizens living in an utterly free society. We delude ourselves if we believe that this occurs only in societies emerging from dictatorships. Anomie is all around us, even and especially in the United States and Western Europe.

I live in an apartment complex in downtown Washington, D.C. It is inhabited primarily by presumably college-educated singles of Generation X. A grimmer lot is hard to imagine. Without a greeting, without a smile, they trot in and out of the building. It's not, one is prepared to allow, that they are hostile. They quite possibly don't even intend to be uncivil. It's just that they are not aware of another's presence—anyone's presence, for that matter, unless one belongs to their particular focus group, professional, sexual, or otherwise.

Have you noticed how people like them run into you on sidewalks, cell phones glued to their ears, oblivious of your existence? Have you noticed, on the other hand, the tragic joylessness of the singles scene that pretends to be so merry? If they were such a happy lot, why would they run a 30 percent higher risk of developing chronic diseases than married people, as one study by the University of Rotterdam has shown?

One of the world's most pathetic singles clubs is in Hamburg, Germany, where an actor dressed as a cardinal weds properly attired pairs "for the evening." This is not really meant to be a joke. When asked why they bothered, many of the couples say earnestly that they "felt a need for this ceremony." Surf the Internet, type "singles" into the search field, and the postmodern world in all its fragmentation will unfold. There are travel agencies that specialize in excursions for Catholic singles, Baptist singles, even vegan singles.

For all the high-minded affirmations of a multicultural society, postmodernity promotes the self and the similar to the detriment of natural—as opposed to ideological—diversity. In reality, postmoderns are by and large incapable of appreciating the wonderful medley of types, vocations, and colors on this earth. Hence, postmodern people have no ground under their feet—less, perhaps, than the niche-dweller under Communism because the niche usually sheltered a variety of refugees from the collectivist untruth that surrounded them.

Proclaiming Christ in this postmodern era includes opening up transcendent realities to men and women. What *do* Christians believe about their Lord?

Christ is the ordering force in the universe. He thus offers Himself as the antidote to fragmentation and postmodern chaos.

Christ is about unity. It is the promise of the Gospel through Baptism that the believer becomes one with Christ and will share His glory. The faithful experience a foretaste of this unity and eternal glory in Holy Communion.

In this unity with Christ and one another, the faithful are genuinely diverse, as the apostle Paul impresses upon Christianity:

> For as in one body we have many members, and all the members do not have the same function, so we, though many, are one body in Christ, and individually members one of another. Having gifts that differ according to the grace given to us, let us use them. (Romans 12:4–6 RSV)

This, then, is the message the church must proclaim ever more clearly to a fragmented generation posing as merry but that is in reality writhing in what the sociologist of religion Peter L. Berger termed "anomic terror."

More than half a century after Dietrich Bonhoeffer's death on the gallows, it has become evident that much of Western humanity senses what he had recognized so early: There is so little ground under our feet. And because there is so little ground, this Gospel of life, then, will at a minimum fall on some open ears.

GETHSEMANE
AND POSTMODERNITY

PAUL HINLICKY

During Holy Week, two categories seem particularly pertinent: power and difference. Postmodern people should know this. People are driven by the vital force within them to establish difference from one another. This results in pervasive relations of domination and submission. Postmoderns have learned to deconstruct the façade of human community along these lines at the feet of teachers who subverted modernity from within.

Marx, Nietzsche, and Freud, each in his own way, dispelled the last illusion, that grandest of all mystifications, that beclouded the sober grasp of the hard truth about life. When the "illusion" of God is abolished in thought, the "true" state of things appears: Hapless human beings are insignificant exponents of a mindless world of eternally recurring collisions of violent force. Violence is scripted into the nature of things. Violence is the ineluctable fact. Deal with it.

The difference between humanity and God, on the other hand, once made all human beings equal in nature before their common Creator and bound them together before His final judgment. The difference was famously expressed in the Declaration of Independence as "self-evident truth," that "all are created equal and endowed by their Creator with certain, inalienable rights . . ." Acknowledgment of the difference was the foundation of modern political institutions of popular sovereignty. (The early moderns prophetically criticized the "divine right" of kings or popes of the premodern regime precisely for obscuring this difference.)

But postmoderns hold no truths, let alone self-evident ones: Human beings are not created, let alone as equals. They are not endowed by a nonexistent Creator with natural rights, let alone definite and inalienable ones, because the nature of things could care less. The impolite and impolitic name of this nay-saying is nihilism. Conscious of this state of affairs, the best attain to a brief flicker of celebrity splendor in an endless cosmic night. But the masses of people are witless cogs in the machine of indifferent nature, driven by one or another mechanism, claimed by its partisans as key to the riddle of human misery: gender, race, class, early childhood neglect, or, lately, rogue genes.

In relentlessly playing out this line of thought, however, postmoderns have discovered an important truth: Discomfort with difference is part and parcel of the extraordinarily vicious violence that has characterized the modern world. The crimes of Hitler, Dresden-Hiroshima, Stalin-Mao-Pol Pot not only dwarf by a vast magnitude whatever previous sins the antecedent religious cultures committed in holy wars and inquisitions, they are qualitatively different *evils* because they have attempted totally to destroy others as "others." Total war, like totalitarianism, is a distinctly modern possibility. This grim insight is at the heart of the postmodern critic of modernism. Many postmoderns want desperately for this tough-minded insight into the connection between difference and violence to be liberating, an insight that frees by teaching us to welcome diversity. But postmoderns find themselves on the horns of a dilemma.

If the perception of difference seems to correlate with violence, how does one welcome difference without inadvertently inviting violence? Ironically, one downplays difference (as only "skin-deep," as merely "cultural") and appeals instead to the common core hedonism of our animal nature. Then all the razzle-dazzle of deconstruction itself deconstructs into a merely libertarian apology for the existing liberal regime. The mantra of "tolerance" becomes the armchair radical's bad faith evasion of the crucial differences in a world where socialization, as they say, "goes all the way down."

By these lights, however, there is no rational way to judge a sincere Nazi as sincerely guilty of holding to an objective moral evil. The postmodern rhetoric of diversity and tolerance has neither norms nor resources to make the move toward nonviolence it earnestly and rightly wishes. It consequently amounts to nothing more than the sentimental piety of the existing order in its advanced state of moral and spiritual decay.

The Christian Scripture also knows something about power and difference. Its key character, God, is *the* difference generating all other differences. The Creator is the author of real distinctions among creatures. Whoever is uncomfortable with difference among creatures is uncomfortable with *the* difference, who differentiates one kind of creature from another. Whoever wants to abolish others in their otherness is quarrelling with the one who is wholly other, to use Rudolf Otto's famous definition of God, the one who indeed stands against us and with all who are other than us whenever we find those others intolerable.

Not that it's an equal contest. God's difference from creatures lies in God's almighty power as Creator of heaven and earth, of all things visible and invisible. God's will, therefore, always prevails in the end, whether we want it to or not. Even rebellion against the will of God is made to serve God's purpose. "You meant it for evil," says the patriarch Joseph to his brothers who had sold him into slavery, "but God meant it for good." (See Genesis 50:15–21.)

This thought of God's overruling reign of a wayward creation is at the heart of the Christian message. Christ is handed over by God "into the hands of sinners"; they mean to destroy Him who has brought God uncomfortably near to them. But in God's wisdom, this act of refusal becomes the occasion of the redemption of those sinners and all other sinners—a sinner being precisely the one who cannot and will not deal with *the* difference, who God is.

One deals with *the* difference, who God is, in prayer. Prayer is not a magical means to power, as superstition has it, but the acknowledgement of God as the one and only Almighty, whose will, though good, is and forever remains other than our own. Prayer thus becomes the existential basis for welcoming others in their otherness and learning to receive them as gifts from above, even when we cannot by our own lights see our human community with them. Prayer takes others on faith.

In this, the prayer of faith follows Christ, learning from Him who prayed in the agony of the Garden of Gethsemane: "Not My will, but Thy will be done!" This prayer is the key to the riddle of history. The drama of human history is the contest between acknowledgment and refusal of God's will for a community of love among genuine others.

This contest has been decided once and for all in Christ the crucified, who in God's name welcomed even sinners, though unworthy, and bore that invitation all the way into our hell of God-forsakeness that we might in its power welcome one another. The Christ of the Gospel surrendered in the Garden of Gethsemane to God's will that He perish in the God-forsaken shame of solidarity with His tormenters, just as if there were no ultimate difference between the persecutors and the persecuted.

That erasure of difference between victim and victimizer in the final court is a stone of stumbling for many. It is perhaps the one good reason (of believing Judaism) not to believe the Christian Gospel, that all have equally sinned and that all may be equally redeemed. But it was also a stone of stumbling for Christ Himself in that agony of prayer in the garden. Surrender meant for Christ Himself a devastating loss of identity, a truth death, which obliterated potentially forever the line between righteousness and sin. Accursed and God-forsaken, yet for love of sinners and in obedience to God, Christ resolved in prayer to perish "reckoned among transgressors."

For those who acknowledge the word of Christ's resurrection on the third day as true, these tremendous contraries were united and transcended in the crucifixion of the Son of God for us. There, God in an act of almighty power obliterated the difference between us. The blind alley of postmodern preoccupation with difference and power might, therefore, yet encounter in Christ the crucified the redemptive alternative path of prayer and righteousness. The power of prayer lies in surrendering to God's almighty will.

The difference this surrender of prayer makes in the world is to constitute new communities of Christ's righteousness, where God is worshiped for God's sake and people know one another as equals in dignity, fulfilling the apostolic word: "For our sake [God] made Him to be sin who knew no sin, so that in [Christ] we might become the righteousness of God" (2 Corinthians 5:21 NRSV).

~~~~~

The Rev. Dr. Paul Hinlicky teaches Christian theology and modern philosophy at Roanoke College, Salem, Virginia.

THE CROSS
AFTER POSTMODERNITY

EBERHARD JÜNGEL

TRANSLATED BY UWE SIEMON-NETTO

What postmodernity? It barely bloomed and has already faded. At least modernity lasted a few centuries. But look at what has happened to its successor. After only a few decades, postmodernity is no longer what it intended or appeared to be. Actually, postmodernity was never able to articulate clearly what it wanted to be. And any effort to mold it into a less-than-ambiguous concept seems quite paradoxical. After all, postmodernity was an affront targeted at any claim to clarity; thus it was ambiguous by definition.

Postmodernity assumed consequence by confronting modernity's ground-in truisms with a multitude of antitheses. Hence, it contrasted modernity's haughty monotony with the desire to discern life in all its colorful facets and then to marvel at them. The postmodern person was one who set out to learn the sense of wonderment all over again after modernity had thoroughly driven it out to teach fear. That's because enlightened modernity had lost an entire dimension—the dimension of mystery as such. This rendered it incapable of awe.

The postmodern person of letters tried to overcome the chasm between the professional and the amateur, a gulf typical for modernism, which was elitist and exclusivist. Therefore, the postmodern person of letters pushed for a pluralism of languages, models, and procedures in one and the same work of literature. Likewise, the postmodern architect combined the most diverse styles in such a way that they wound up commenting, mocking, and relativizing one another.

Postmodern thinkers experienced a breathtaking acceleration in the acquisition of knowledge. They experienced the speed with which ever-new interpretations of the respective stocks of knowledge were chasing each other. These experiences freed them to relativize themselves. And this in turn even made modernity appear less obsolete than the multitude of antitheses to its plausibilities suggested. The long and the short of this is that postmodernity allots to every era its genuine right and engages in a direct relationship with all times.

Having said this, one is tempted to establish all kinds of analogies between the ways postmodernity and the Christian faith define themselves. Does not the New Testament invite and exhort the world to believe in Jesus as the one who is Lord not only over the present, but over all times? "Jesus Christ is the same yesterday and today and forever" (Hebrews 13:8 NRSV). Is not the Lord's apostle, a master in many language games, just as much a Law-abiding Jew to the Jews as a lawless individual to the lawless and a weak man to the weak? Has Paul not become everything to everybody to save some by every means possible? (See 1 Corinthians 9:2ff.)

Surely Christianity would be in a position to masquerade as postmodern. It could well do so if it were not for the Gospel's trenchant claim to truth. This claim is so trenchant that Paul defiantly told Peter, the prince of the apostles, to his face that he was acting contrary to Gospel truth (Galatians 2:11). In New Testament parlance, coming to faith is synonymous with acquiring truth. Postmodern people, on the other hand, know no unambiguous claim to truth. Like Pilate, they ask with masterful irony: "What is truth?" (John 18:38 NRSV).

The New Testament's answer to this question also seems almost ironic. At any rate, it impresses the reader as quite silly. Thus Paul has called it a "foolishness to Gentiles" and a "stumbling block to Jews" (1 Corinthians 1:23 NRSV). This truth consists of the statement that the eternal and almighty God has come to this world as a human person, that He has been executed in the name of the Law as a lawfully condemned criminal. This had to strike the religious world as a scandal and a folly.

What? The cross is good news? Friedrich Nietzsche claimed that this meant turning all values of antiquity on their head. Nietzsche said that this God created by Paul amounted to the denial of a god. Indeed, it must seem absurd to the postmodern way of thinking that God, the Highest of the highest, should be capable of such self-degradation.

Natural reason perceives God, if it thinks of Him at all, in the way Anselm of Canterbury (1033–1109) did: God is that beyond which nothing greater can be thought of. The cross of Jesus Christ teaches us a different view: If the Highest of the highest identifies with an executed man, then it is evidently a true attribute of divine majesty that He can also humble Himself. This is why Martin Luther balanced the statement "Nothing is so great; God is still greater" with another statement: "Nothing is so small, God is still smaller."

Yet this dialectic does not exhaust the Gospel's truth. I may admire this dialectic, but it does not necessarily affect me. The point of the Gospel's truth is concrete. It is directed at my own existence. The point of the Gospel is that God in the person of Jesus Christ participates in our death so we may participate in His life. On the cross God is not only one of us, but He actually takes our place. This is where He suffers what none of us is capable of enduring: the weight of human guilt and the curse of human Godlessness.

This has been ridiculed and opposed as divine masochism. It is hard to conceive of a more foolish misinterpretation of Christ's vicarious suffering and death, which, mind you, seemed foolish already to the Gentiles. The masochist seeks suffering for the sake of suffering. But the crucified one has suffered the appalling force of death and all the powers of destruction to free suffering humanity from their sway. He was capable of doing this only because God Himself was acting. Ever since, Christians have been singing:

> It was a strange and dreadful strife
> When life and death contended;
> The victory remained with life,
> The reign of death was ended.
> Holy Scripture plainly says,
> That death is swallowed up by death,
> Its sting is lost forever.
> Alleluia!
> (Martin Luther, "Christ Jesus Lay in Death's Strong Bands")

Death is still around, of course, inflicting deep wounds on the world every day. But it will not be victorious. It is "swallowed up in victory" (1 Corinthians 15:54 NRSV). The Gospel is the message of victory, a message intended to reach the entire world. It gives us a new understanding of God. It makes us see God as the source of all life, who is even capable of suffering death. In this unity of life and death that ultimately results in life, God is none other than love.

This message of victory makes us see ourselves in a new light. Indeed, it places us in a new venue where we experience ourselves as liberated from life's lies. There, we enjoy an existence as new people who receive every morning our lives anew from a yet unspent future that feeds on God's eternity. On Easter morning, this *Urbild* (archetype) of the new person became reality. He who believes in the resurrected one and has faith in Him will experience the sovereign indicative of grace, "so if anyone is in Christ, there is a new creation: everything old has passed away; see, everything has become new!" (2 Corinthians 5:17 NRSV). This indicative of grace, then, opens the way forward and puts us on this road—without our contributing to this endeavor. In the trail of the resurrected one, the believing person receives and spreads the freedom that swings beyond this world.

Then this freedom swings back just as powerfully to everyday life with its duties and woes. Duties? To those who know the sovereign indicative of grace, our everyday duties cannot be anything but imperatives of freedom, liberated from the dictatorship of the Law whose requirements God has written on our hearts (Romans 2:15), a Law that challenges and often overtaxes us.

These imperatives feed from grace and instruct the believer in the right use of freedom. They do not scorn civic morality, but they point beyond all morality. These imperatives direct believers to a life in which they can forget themselves and do what should be self-evident. In this way they mirror Christ, who "emptied Himself, taking the form of a slave" (Philippians 2:7 NRSV) and in doing so was glorified.

At least in light of this dialectic, postmodernity ought to gain a new vitality and develop a new sense of wonderment in an entirely different manner. There is more to discover here than colorful aspects of the lives we live. The grace of God is itself colorful and "varied" (1 Peter 4:10). This colorful grace breaks through the grayness of our everyday lives. And once in a while, the original colors of creation shimmer through.

This is why the way of thinking this wonderment has put in motion is not intent on putting a rational end to wonderment as quickly as possible. It was the great Aristotle who postulated putting a rational end to wonderment as a philosophical goal. But the opposite is true. The way of thinking that is focused on the Word of the cross leads us deeper and deeper into wonderment. This way of thinking concentrates on a mystery that becomes even more mysterious the better one understands it: the mystery of divine love that is capable of suffering and, for this reason, capable of renewal.

~~~~~

The Rev. Dr. Eberhard Jüngel, a Lutheran theologian, is director of the Institute of Hermeneutics, Tübingen University, Germany.

THE EUCHARIST VS. POSTMODERN CHAOS

ROBERT P. IMBELLI

W illiam Butler Yeat's "The Second Coming" contains what are, arguably, the most-quoted lines of twenti-eth-century poetry: "Things fall apart; the centre cannot hold; Mere anarchy is loosed upon the world." Written in 1920, the poem not only summed up the horror of the still young century, it seemed prescient of horrors yet to come. I have a particularly poignant association with these lines. I remember that they were invoked by Robert Kennedy in an article he wrote shortly before his assassination in 1968, an event that precipitated a further descent into the anarchy the poet foresaw.

Postmodernity may be, to some degree, a pretentious academic fad. But its soil is undoubtedly the collapse of an authoritative, life-giving center and the ensuing fragmenta-tion experienced daily in culture, politics, and individual lives. One result is the emergence of the "protean self," which is imaginatively portrayed in Woody Allen's film *Zelig*. Here is the self without a center, blending effortlessly into the most disparate situations and bound by no ultimate and lasting commitments.

But, alas, the self is also quite capable of murderous rage and unloosing destruction. Brooding over the new century is no longer the specter of Marx but that of Nietzsche. The "death of God" leads to an abyss of nothingness. While many strive to fill the emptiness with the ever-changing trinkets of consumerism or the endless titillations of the media, a few do so by indulging an unfettered will to power. And over all, absence reigns.

Faced with this cultural situation (one that Pope John Paul II has called a "culture of death"), where is the Christian believer to find, in the words of another poet, T. S. Eliot, "the still point of the turning world"? Ultimately we find it in the Eucharist, the flaming center of the world, the Sacrament of Real Presence. At the central point of the Roman Catholic celebration of the Eucharist, the priest exhorts the congregation: "Let us proclaim the mystery of faith." And the congregation exclaims: "Christ has died, Christ is risen, Christ will come again." In doing so the faithful trace the temporal coordinates of the new world of faith.

"Christ has died." The Eucharist celebrates, remembers, represents the once and for all sacrifice of Christ on Calvary. Christ descended into the abyss of death, the void of absence. He attained new and everlasting life not despite death but by transforming death. Thus Christ's followers are schooled in the Eucharist not to deny death in its many forms—such as disappointment, hardship, failure—but, in company with Christ, to transform the power of death.

For "Christ is risen." The Christ present in the Eucharist is the living Jesus, and the disciples live through Him and with Him and in Him. He is not a dim figure of the past to be studied at a distance, but He is the living one encountered in the today of faith. Christ declares: "I am the first and the last, and the living one; I died, and behold I am alive for evermore, and I have the keys of Death and Hades" (Revelation 1:17–18 RSV). In the Eucharist we do not learn about Christ, but we learn from Him.

Still Christ's presence remains hidden under sacramental signs. It is a real presence that is not yet fully manifest. So faith confesses that "Christ will come again" to sum up all things in Himself, to "judge the living and the dead." Only then will He complete the work of creation and redemption and "God may be all in all" (1 Corinthians 15:28 NRSV).

The Eucharist opens to faith a new world of persons in relation, persons whose form and substance is the person of Jesus Christ. It also calls forth the new personhood of the participants, their gradual transformation as living members of Christ's body. "Here there cannot be Greek and Jew, circumcised and uncircumcised, barbarian, Scythian, slave, free man, but Christ is all and in all" (Colossians 3:11 RSV).

The whole thrust of the Eucharist is to nurture a movement from fragmentation to integration: The broken bread becomes the salvific means for the gathering in of the many; the blood outpoured achieves the being "one" of the world. What is de-centered finds its center in the Eucharist. Those who despair of meaning can find here God's meaning and purpose.

The Eucharist, then, is pure gift, it is grace. God so loved the world that He gives His only Son. And the Son so loves that He continues to give Himself for the world's salvation, nowhere more tangibly than in the Eucharist. And the recipient can only exclaim: "What wondrous love is this, O my soul!"

But the Eucharist is also imperative, a task. It calls believers, nourished and equipped by Christ, to transform both themselves and their world. In place of the protean, rootless self of postmodernity, the Eucharist fosters a centered self, free to give generously as he or she has so generously received. What better name for this self who emerges from the encounter with Christ in the Eucharist than a "eucharistic self," one whose native language is thanksgiving? As Paul writes to the Colossians: "Whatever you do, in word or deed, do everything in the name of the Lord Jesus, giving thanks to God the Father through Him" (3:17 RSV).

The deeds that flow from such a eucharistic self are deeds of service in solidarity with the most needy members of Christ's body. The participants in the Eucharist are sent forth to undertake works of justice and peace that help provide the human conditions for genuine thanksgiving. The eminently practical Epistle of James warns: "If a brother or sister is ill-clad and in lack of daily food, and one of you says to them, 'Go in peace, be warmed and filled,' without giving them the things needed for the body, what does it profit?" (2:15–16 RSV).

The Eucharist both nourishes a eucharistic self and promotes a eucharistic ethic. As is well known, the account of the Last Supper in the Gospel of John does not contain a narrative of the institution of the Eucharist, as the other Gospels do. In its place we find, instead, Jesus washing the feet of His disciples and instructing them: "I have given you an example, that you also should do as I have done to you" (John 13:15 RSV).

Therefore, the injunction of Christ, "Do this in memory of Me," repeated at every celebration of the Eucharist, embraces both the breaking of the bread and ongoing service to others. Both these eucharistic actions are performed for the life of the world, for the fuller realization of Christ's presence among us.

~~~~

The Rev. Dr. Robert P. Imbelli, a priest of the Catholic Archdiocese of New York, teaches theology at Boston College.

CHRIST'S COMEBACK
IN ART

THEODORE L. PRESCOTT

If a picture is worth a thousand words, there is no shortage of talk in the third millennium after Christ's birth. We sometimes are told that our world is in the midst of a revolution of consciousness because our communications are so predominantly visual. It's hard to argue with that idea, given the torrent of print, electronic, film, and outdoor pictures to which we are subjected each day. The multiplication and mutation of images has not necessarily made communication easier, though. This revolution in consciousness has come with a cost. What is both intriguing and unsettling about our time is how malleable images and words have become.

In fact, some postmodern thinkers have argued that we live in a universe of free-floating signs and images, where meanings are in flux and essentially arbitrary. In their thought, the old idea that people could truly understand themselves and one another and that some truths could be communicated across vast differences in time and culture is naïve or foolish.

One of the hallmarks of postmodern art has been a kind of mix-and-mismatch approach to images. If modern artists viewed the forms and traditions of the past with disdain as they sought progress, postmodern artists have often treated the past as a kind of big clip-art book, a source for cool effects, jarring relocations, and ironic contrasts.

While postmodernity's roots stretch into the 1960s, the full effects were first seen in the art and architecture of the 1980s. The effects were not limited to museums, galleries, and buildings in large metropolitan areas; instead, they quickly spread to strip malls, car dealerships, and retail outlets. The lumberyard in my small Pennsylvania town built a new store in the mid-1980s. The store is a ribbed metal industrial building, spare and utilitarian. But its entrance is framed by a colonnade of imposing Corinthian columns. They are chrome yellow plastic and support only a primer red entablature. The building is "fun," and it cheekily calls attention to its business by joining a ubiquitous industrial shed to a garish rendition of a venerable Greek architectural order.

Religious subjects and convictions were not prominent in modern art. Apart from some abstract artists, such as Mark Rothko, who had transcendental aspirations, or earnest "primitives," such as Edgar Tolson, religion was largely banished from modern art's consciousness. It was one of the first casualties of modernism's reductive understanding of progress. This changed as postmodern artists challenged the orthodoxies of modern art and began to explore its taboos.

Thus in the 1980s and 1990s, the characters, signs, and symbols of many historic world religions began to appear again in art after more than a century of absence. Saints, angels, and crucifixes jostled with Hindu gods and spirit beings from the Caribbean. There was no particular style associated with these religious references, though the artists, who are loosely known as Neo-Expressionists and who include the German painter Anselm Kiefer, seemed particularly attracted to religiously suggestive subjects.

It was at this time that critics and artists began to discuss art in terms of "spirituality," which continues to be a widely used term. This spirituality is intensely personal and appears to affirm belief without being specific about its nature. This kind of spirituality also reveals the religious content of postmodern art to be highly individualistic, with little or no relationship to institutional religion. This is particularly true for the Christian church, which has stood removed from the centers of art for the past 200 years.

For people who like to "get" the meaning of art, it has often been difficult to see what the religious references in postmodern art have signified. In the work of some artists, it suggests an openness to the supernatural and the conviction that there is more to life than biology or politics. Other postmodernists seem to use religious images to add a dash of mystery and romance to otherwise lackluster work. But it has not been difficult to see that the most notorious postmodern work employing Christian imagery seemed calculated to offend, and it stood opposed to historic belief.

The adherents of the mix-and-mismatch philosophy were apparently surprised and alarmed to discover that some people really cared about what images mean. One does not need to have been close to the art scene to have heard noise from the battles known as the "culture wars." One such eruption occurred in 1999 over a painting by a young British artist that was included in an exhibition at the Brooklyn Museum. The work that caused the uproar was a painting of the Virgin Mary titled *Sensations* that included elephant dung as one of the ingredients of the painting.

The shock value of *Sensations* was promoted by the museum, which developed "warning" advertisements that said exposure to the exhibit might induce nausea and vomiting. Clearly the museum was banking on the enduring premodern belief that controversy would stimulate attendance. They were not disappointed. For many Christians and indeed for many "ordinary" citizens, the controversies surrounding postmodern artists' use of Christian images are proof of the corruption of art in our age.

Thus "postmodern" is often used to mean hollow, cynical, exploitative, and opposed to Christian conviction. There is certainly plenty of evidence to support this view. However, all of the attention to controversy has hidden a quieter change in art that is in some sense postmodern too. The postmodern assault on the rules and taboos of modern art gave artists the opportunity to take a fresh look at the roots of Western art. One does not have to travel far back toward those roots to discover a wealth of Christian images.

While some artists have lifted those images out of their context and treated them without regard for their meaning, other artists have found the ideas and stories of Christianity to have a magnetic pull in a different direction. The biblical accounts of human grandeur, folly, tragedy, sin, and redemption speak to something essential in the human condition.

Some artists have been moved by their contact with the past and have begun a journey toward faith. Recently I learned that a prominent figurative painter, who has been delving into religious subjects for some time, has started to identify himself with the faith and with the church. Probably the most underreported development in art during the rise of postmodernity is the growing number of artists who are followers of Christ. Their work crosses all the genres and styles of contemporary art, thus there is no art movement in the way that one is usually defined. But their presence is slowly being acknowledged.

At the time in the liturgical calendar when churches throughout the world celebrate the resurrection of Jesus

Christ, Christians might do well to ponder the cultural implications of Christ's life, death, and resurrection. It is easy to see our cultural moment in terms of its death because there are so many destructive forces at work in the arts. However, it is entirely possible that a vital art, leavened by faith, may arise from the ashes of postmodern culture.

~~~~~

Prof. Theodore L. Prescott is teaching art at Messiah College, Grantham, Pennsylvania.

SCIENCE POINTS TO GOD

OLIVERA PETROVICH

The postmodern society has passionately sought to convince us of our freedom to choose standards and values by which to live. Yet the choices that most of us make are neither whimsical nor infinitely diverse. To dismiss our adherence to certain common values as no more than human desire to conform to social norms would be both superficial and psychologically naïve. However chaotic the world may seem to have become, psychological research suggests that human beings are born with mechanisms or "expectations" by means of which already in infancy we begin to learn about and understand how our universe works.

We grasp not only the observable features of the universe, but also those features that can only be inferred by us because of their fundamentally invisible nature. An example of the latter is our concepts of the divine. The interplay in our knowledge between the concepts of the observable (objects and events), on the one hand, and the unobservable (underlying principles), on the other, underpins scientific as well as metaphysical accounts of the world.

Denial of such principles by postmodern thought could be a symptom of exasperation and intellectual exhaustion that results from our often misplaced search for proofs. Children, like most ordinary adults, do not show signs of such frustration nor do they succumb to the challenges of relativism. Indeed, the adequacy of perception and reason as tools for understanding the world around us have been taken for granted throughout human religious history and were later corroborated by modern psychological research.

In this regard, the Bible and scientific psychology tell the same story, albeit in different ways. Its moral is that paying attention to the surrounding world with an open mind reliably gives rise to spiritual insight. St. Paul, for example, is quite explicit that humans can have knowledge of God from creation (Romans 1: 20). A few centuries later St. Antony the Great likewise proclaims that "It is not difficult to gain spiritual understanding of God. If you wish to contemplate Him, look at the providential harmony in all the things created by His Logos" (*Philokalia*, 1:353). Even Immanuel Kant's stark analysis of the limits of human reason to ascertain God's existence failed to destroy the philosopher's own sense of awe at the sight of "the starry heavens above . . . and the moral law within" (*Critique of Practical Reason*, 5:161–62).

Numerous informal records testify that the natural world elicits a similar response in children. In my recent studies in Britain and Japan, virtually every child that I have tested could articulate this connection by the time they were 4 years old. What is striking about those findings is that the Japanese culture excludes any concepts of transcendent causality from its religious system, yet in their own understanding of the world, ordinary individuals manifestly postulate a divine creator. The same pattern of reasoning was observed in Japanese adults who were tested as a comparison group. In short, regardless of their age and culture, humans perceive the physical world in the same fundamental categories of natural kinds and artifacts, reflect on what they perceive, and draw remarkably similar inferences about its origin and structure.

This common rational core is the very quality of our nature that Christ was addressing when He appealed to our readiness to recognize the divine in simple objects and events and by our basic psychological processes. "Look at the birds of the air . . ."; "See how the lilies in the field grow . . ."; "Listen to another parable . . .," says Jesus to the disciples and to the crowds.

Religious thinkers from diverse traditions and epochs, those preceding Christ as well as His followers (whether Catholic, Orthodox, or Reformed), appeal to the same core ability of human cognition to infer the supernatural from the natural. To the ancient Athenians, the Creator was "An Unknown God" because they understood that this God did not dwell in the temples made by human hands (Acts 17:23–24).

All these examples from human religious history are consistent with findings from psychological research, each suggesting that something in our cognitive nature remains constant and ageless despite the many cultural influences that interfere with its expression. One clear implication of cognitive-psychological research is that a radical postmodernist distinction between old and new ways of thinking is untenable. Certain ways of thinking are inherent in the human constitution and undergo little development from childhood to adulthood.

Consistencies in cognitive development, together with the consistencies observed in the physical world, explain why the knowledge constructed by humans throughout their development is neither random nor capricious. Instead, it reveals discernible patterns that are best observed when large numbers of individuals are examined. Such systematic and purposeful comparisons of individuals across different cultures can reveal important underlying similarities in a number of conceptual domains.

By contrast, postmodern methods of inquiry do not tell us anything about the psychological processes that give rise to cultural diversity because such methods focus on the products of the author's thought (usually texts) rather than the thought itself. To understand the author's perspective, however, psychology requires that we examine the author and not only his or her texts and other created products. When we do so, we are forced to take notice of evidence that our psychological processes are not incommensurably different from person to person but share important common characteristics.

Consequently, the postmodern emphasis on the uniqueness of each person's encounter with external reality, which entails a denial of any objective truth, only appears plausible in the absence of actual data about the nature of human cognitive development. For this reason, somewhat anarchic, even frightening, implications of postmodernism pose no threat to human rational capacity and the intrinsic tendency to search for meaning and coherence. It is hardly surprising that postmodernism has had no impact on cognitive-developmental psychology and scientific psychology in general.

There may, however, be another way to look at the fundamental tenets of postmodernism. Its insistence on the plurality of perspectives and methods as the only way to understand religious phenomena in postmodern times is, perhaps, an implicit recognition that there is something in common to all this apparent variety. While postmodernism has brought a flood of modern religions, giving each person freedom and encouragement to communicate with the divine in his or her own unique way, it would be misguided to infer from this that each person also conceptualizes God in a unique and unpredictable way.

In view of the evidence mentioned above, it is clear that there are conditions under which individuals from markedly different religious traditions demonstrate at least one common religious concept, that of a creator. Such evidence runs counter to widespread stereotypes about the alleged incommensurability between the ways of thinking among people from vastly different cultures.

~~~~~

Dr. Olivera Petrovich, an Orthodox Christian, teaches psychology at Oxford University.

LET THE SEARCH BEGIN

WILLIAM MURCHISON

Postmo-*what*? Numerous members of the media I joined nearly four decades ago—an institution then known quaintly as the press—would have hoo-hah'ed that formulation. Questing hands might well have slid to the bottom-left desk drawer, emerging with a half-consumed bottle of rye: just the thing for a toast to the latest piece of Harvard-sounding jargon. Postmodernity! Sure, sure. It was a different time, a different institution, one with little tolerance for intellectual pretense. Around the newsroom, district attorneys and police sergeants were better-liked figures than senators and political spinmeisters.

My brothers (the calling was still mainly male) with the cigarette ash on their worn coat sleeves were in large degree conservative populists. I still dazzle the young people with tales of how the denizens of my newsroom in the 1960s laughed at hippies and jeered at war protesters. But you know, that was then, and this is now. In no small way the media are at the center of our postmodernity perplexities. They will tell us what they think it is good for us to know.

They will tell us, moreover, the meaning of what they have told us.

Our focus in these essays is Jesus Christ. The old media, the press, would have regarded that focus as natural. Just as the community regarded itself broadly, and at times a little vaguely, as Christian, so the press partook of that commitment. Newspaper publishers were active in churches (but out of charity one did not probe too deeply for motive). A goodly number of journalists went to church. Saturday "church pages" were common, sometimes running sermon texts. The mastheads of certain newspapers, generally in small towns, carried Bible passages.

As its Christmas lead editorial, one major southwestern daily ran verbatim the nativity account from St. Luke; the off, or second, lead was from the first chapter of St. John's Gospel—the Word made flesh, dwelling among us with grace and truth. Thus the Christian Gospel received from at least one organ of journalism a public thump on the back, which was not entirely a bad thing, I thought then and think now. In the main, the media wanted readers to know that, like them, they endorsed Christianity, or if they did not endorse every minute detail of its doctrines, at least they endorsed its spirit.

What is left of this state of affairs? Not much, in all conscience. Coverage of religious news today draws in the Muslims and the practitioners of New Age ways—including Wicca. At the newspaper of which I previously spoke, St. Luke and St. John yielded almost two decades ago to a string of editorial page vignettes concerning the daily good deeds of unsung heroes. Of course it would be absurd to say that Christianity goes unrecognized. The point for reflection is that it goes uncelebrated, unsingled-out, for approbation or praise. This is the case for at least three basic reasons.

1. Under the postmodern regime, singling out one religion for recognition over another seems unfair and unreasonable. If

glimmers of truth may be found in all religions, we can't throw the newspaper's authority behind one version via editorial endorsement. Well, can we? To say that we can, and should, endorse one truth would suggest antidemocratic bias in favor of the convictions (never mind how historic or widespread) of only some Americans when what we want is to affirm all Americans, sparing necessary reproofs for those who press their agendas too hard—for example, Christian fundamentalists. (Christian fundamentalists, especially those with guns in their homes or cigarettes in their mouths, may be the last remaining bad guys in postmodern America. That is what comes of believing too strongly in objective, unvarying truth.)

2. Media organs are businesses. Businesses respect their customers. The postmodern convictions of many contemporary customers prevent the media from pressing the truth button too hard. Don't Wiccans subscribe to newspapers and watch TV? Don't Muslims? Mightn't these valued customers object if Jesus received undue attention as the incarnate Son of God?

3. In any case, Christian conviction doesn't exactly reverberate through today's media. Most of the old Christian publishers (e.g., Henry Luce) long ago were taken up by the same Lord they professed to worship. Media companies are run today by executive committees, which hardly regard religious conviction as a criterion for membership. No longer do reporters go to church except to cover celebrity funerals. A survey some 20 years ago said something like 90 percent of "elite" media figures never darkened a church door. Thus the situation is that secularists—not theists and certainly not Christians—largely decide what is news and how that news will be covered.

As one might suppose, Christianity—still the world's largest religion—receives less respectful treatment from the media than was formerly the case. That same numerical preponderance may actually weigh against respectful treatment. Whereas the media would be loath to pick on less numerous, and presumably more helpless, "faith communities" such as the Jews and the Muslims, Christians are seen as big boys and girls, well able to look after themselves.

Big or not, Christianity seems to invite increasing hostility, especially from that portion of the media whose focus is entertainment. Catholic priests, prolife activists, anti-pornography campaigners, and southern evangelicals know that part of the weight of the cross they bear in postmodernity consists in ridicule—duly retailed by the media. It needs to be pointed out that the media do not actively oppose and work to subvert Christianity (though the activities of particular media figures might convey exactly that impression).

The salient consideration is that Christianity has become just one more creed, one more lifestyle, among many requiring coverage. How dare Christians assert a demand for preference? I suppose that, speaking as a member both of the media and the Christian faith community, I should feel discouraged at prospects for the future. Well, some sentimental regret possibly is indicated but not much more.

Between what is essential and what is merely nice lies a world of difference. Yes, it was nice that the media used to serve with their lips the conviction that Christianity was true. That truth, asserted by Christians throughout the ages, was never dependent upon its reception and presentation in what passed in given epochs for the communications industry. If what you profess and teach is true, the withdrawal of belief or commitment cannot subtract from that truth. It can make harder and more intense the job of proclamation, but that is all.

The media's sociable taste for Christianity was never the whole show for Christians; it was a means to an end— the wider embrace of God's saving love in Jesus Christ. Come to think of it, in *The Sound of Music,* one of the media's more famous, if light-as-a-feather, backpats for Christianity, there occurs what you might call a watchword for the present moment. Julie Andrews says, "When the Lord closes a door, somewhere He opens a window."

Not bad. *Bang!* goes the door through which the media once reverently ushered Christians to the best seats in the house. Where's that window now, that new means of access to hearts and souls and minds? Some searching may be necessary, some climbing. Who can say the result won't be worth the labor?

~~~~~

William Murchison is a Dallas-based syndicated columnist.

PRAYER:
A VERTICAL ACTIVITY

UWE SIEMON-NETTO

Shall we pray? Shall we meditate? Shall we stretch out on the analyst's couch and bare our souls? Varied are the options to cater to our spiritual needs in postmodern times, an era whose mark is mushiness. Postmodernists don't like to make distinctions they may not be able to maintain. Perhaps they say, "What's the difference?" Perhaps, though, this is the right time to bring clarity into this era of spiritual confusion.

Since the early days of the church, the Sundays between Easter and Pentecost have been identified by wonderful Latin names: *Quasimodogeniti* (as newborn babes), *Misericordias Domini* (mercy of the Lord), *Jubilate* (rejoice!), *Cantate* (sing!), *Rogate* (pray!), and *Exaudi* (listen!). This essay is about *Rogate*, so let us consider for a moment an activity that Martin Luther called the "highest service of Christendom, next to preaching."

To Christians, Jews, and Muslims, preaching and praying are intertwined: Through the preacher God speaks to us, and in prayer we talk to God. But there is one important difference in this respect between the three monotheistic religions. For Jews and Christians, prayer is an act of obedience to the First Commandment. It is, however, perfectly in order to shout at God in despair, as long as we acknowledge Him as Lord.

After the terrorist attacks of September 11, 2001, a Boston rabbi scandalized an imam in a television debate by pointing out that as children of God we are within our rights when we grumble. "After all," the rabbi said, "more than one-third of the Psalms are complaints." The Islamic cleric was horrified: "No! This is not permissible!"

Well, to those who listened carefully, this one exclamation spoke volumes about a stark contrast between seemingly similar faiths. A Muslim's relationship with the divine is that of submission to Allah; that is what the word *Islam* means. Jews and Christians, on the other hand, see human beings as God's cooperators, to quote Luther. They argue prayerfully with the senior partner, who, Christians profess, even humbles Himself for our salvation.

This distinction tends to get lost in the current religious *ratatouille*, just as confusing prayer and meditation—the latter preferably practiced with an Eastern flair—is a property of postmodernity. This is not to belittle meditation; it's that meditation is something entirely different. We might meditate on a sacred text. We might look inward to our deepest depth, presumably a helpful exercise, though we can never be quite sure what we'll find. From a theological perspective, meditation is a downward form of contemplation.

And far be it from me to make light of psychoanalysis, which is helpful when well executed. But it is a craft that falls into the realm of anthropology; it does not deal with God. Psychoanalysis is a horizontal business, as *Jake's Women*, an amusing television comedy, taught us years ago. The show was about an author whose imagination was such that he could project the women of his life into the present at any given moment. His sister, his daughter, his former wives, and his analyst entered his reality, arguing, flirting, laughing, crying with him, making his bed. For the purposes of this essay, the analyst was the most noteworthy. She said, "Did you not know that psychoanalysis cannot really heal you? It just makes you feel better between sessions."

No theologian could have said it better. Theologically speaking, psychoanalysis is a level business because it deals with a horizontal existence—the soul. It is horizontal in the sense that by its very nature it cannot reach upward to God. The soul has to make do with the gifts specific to the secular realm: natural law, Mosaic law, and medicine—or, in this case, the competence of a psychiatrist or psychologist. It is an anthropological, not a theological, category.

In New Testament Greek, it is not the word *psyche* that describes absolute being and the immortal self. The expression for this is *zoe*, a term the evangelist John uses to define eternal life. John quotes Christ as saying, "I am the way, and the truth, and the life [*zoe*]" (John 14:6 NRSV). *Zoe*, then, is life as a fruit of faith, through which alone human beings can reach God. *Zoe* is a theological factor. It is absolute being and, therefore, vertical because it is connected with God.

Like eternal life, prayer points upward. It is a dialogue with God, who responds to it as He responds to the weeping of a child (Genesis 21:16–17). A praying person does not contemplate his or her soul but becomes intimate with the Creator, praises Him, gives Him thanks, calls on Him, petitions Him, sometimes argues with Him, confesses to Him, asks for His pardon, and rejoices: "Blessed be God, because He has not rejected my prayer or removed His steadfast love from me" (Psalm 66:20 NRSV).

Prayer is communication with God without pretense, without phony piety. The Bible does not prescribe how, where and in what position this is to be done. No couch, no lotus seat, is necessary. "Whenever you pray, go into your room and shut the door and pray to your Father, who is in secret; and your Father who sees in secret will reward you," Christ advised His followers before teaching them the Lord's Prayer (Matthew 6:6–16 NRSV).

Ultimately, God Himself informs prayer, the apostle Paul teaches. This excludes self-serving prayers, but it includes intercession, which is praying for others. Thus *Rogate* is a countercultural day because intercession is not on the contemporary agenda. Intercession requires altruism, and without it there is no *zoe*, no upward traffic to God, no absolute existence.

It is this message that makes the Sunday of *Rogate* so important for our era because it points a way out of the postmodern quagmire.

DRESDEN BISHOPS IN DIALOGUE

VOLKER KRESS AND JOACHIM REINELT

TRANSLATED BY UWE SIEMON-NETTO

The Lutheran and Catholic bishops of Dresden debate the future of faith in postmodern times.

Bishop Reinelt (Catholic): Until 1990, the Communist system drove many into isolation. It was hard to find a community where people could lay themselves open. At times only small Christian groups and active congregations afforded their members this opportunity. The bulk of the population conducted their lives to suit their personal interests. This often led to a sense of isolation and a yearning for community.

Bishop Kress (Lutheran): The society of the G.D.R (German Democratic Republic) was called a society of niches for a very good reason. People sought their niches in a variety of ways. The church itself was a niche. To some extent this was quite a cozy existence; it strengthened and comforted the church. But the church could not maintain a lively contact with the majority of the population. The state saw to that. Thus many looked for other niches. This broke the bond that had been instrumental in keeping human beings together in the past.

Reinelt: The party imposed the collective, robbing the individual of independence. This has caused a desire to restore common goals for the entire society. That was the true meaning of the enthusiastic cry in 1989, "We are one people." In isolation one always yearns for community.

Kress: First, they shouted, "We want out of here!" Then others, especially Christians, replied, "We stay!" Following that came the powerful cry of the revolutionary month of October 1989: "We are *the* people." What followed was the statement, "We are *one* people." This last shout surfaced to a yearning for a reunified Germany—and for the concocted image of a prosperous world. So now we have to cope with that prosperous world's problems.

Reinelt: For the second time, we are now witnessing a temptation to go it alone: Make a life for yourself; make it as comfortable, as pleasant, as independent, and as emancipated as possible. This challenges us to respond to postmodernity with a new way of thinking. It is impossible to arbitrarily give life a new meaning. We must point to the direction God has given us in Christ. We can't afford to once again opt for isolation, albeit one that is more elegant than its predecessor. We must open up to one another.

Kress: An excessive sense of liberty has replaced the niches. Postmodernity's worst defects are self-realization and a selfish lifestyle, evidently even in the church. People do not really seek community at worship. They seek personal religious experience without inner commitment.

Reinelt: And because of that, the essential thing we require to be truly human has gone astray: giving ourselves to others. This is the core of the Christian message; it is the essence of what Christ has done. To be faithful to God the Father and self-giving to others was the very content of His life. Christians believe that we are created and redeemed to live according to this pattern. Therefore, we only achieve our goal if we accept this core of the Gospel. Our Lord affirmed that the two great commands are to love God and love others. This is where the deepest longing of humanity comes into its own. This is our way; there is none other.

Kress: I am not so sure that this is the deepest longing of human beings. From my experiences, we do not seem that wistful, alas. At any rate, this longing is one of humanity's imperatives, given by God. Not only the Gospel tells us this. The term *justice* permeates the Old Testament, justice in the sense of one's own participation: How do I participate in this life in God's power and reign? Hence, the notion of community is embodied in the concept of justice, which makes it a central tenet of Christianity.

Reinelt: If our lives do not reflect this central tenet, we will be unhappy. We keep deceiving ourselves when we seek happiness in all the wrong places. Bitter disappointments follow. For example, no person can be everything for me. We all have our limits. Work, wealth, beauty and health are not everything. We have been created for something greater.

Kress: I agree. The most rewarding moments in life occur when one hands over part of oneself for others. As a rule, the so-called dark periods of life are often the most blessed. Even secularized people experience this. Sometimes I am in awe of people without faith in such times. Suddenly they discover the inward profoundness of life and live accordingly to the extent that others recognize it. We can only lead a full and profound life when others participate in it.

143

Reinelt: Community happens through pain, suffering, and the cross, when one carries the other's burden. We must not feel sorry that disappointments, destitution, fear, and even death still exist. If we are most intensively challenged to give ourselves, we will experience final greatness. This is all the more so because in giving ourselves we become, in reality, recipients. In following the cross, we become icons of the Trinity because we do not remain with the cross, but we partake in the Father's glory through the resurrected Christ.

Kress: The cross is indeed a wonderful sign that everybody ultimately can experience. I fondly remember an aunt who told me, "Everybody encounters God once in his life, at least once." This occurs especially as one experiences the cross. This is why I believe that this ancient symbol of Christianity will remain an irreplaceably valid sign that nothing can push aside.

Reinelt: What your aunt has said is so comforting! She relates the kind of optimism our postmodern world requires. Everyone in every country is given a chance for a new beginning.

Kress: The churches in this secularized country are in danger of writing off the others and retreating into their own fortress. If we do that, we ignore God's will that everybody be saved. He wants all to recognize the truth. And this is not something that is in our hands—everybody has their opportunity and their hour with God. And we do experience astonishing things. Just think of the thousands that assemble in the Christmas season for Vesper services in front the Church of Our Lady [a large Lutheran church that was destroyed in the devastating air raid on Dresden in early 1945 and is being rebuilt]. As a ruin, this church was a symbol of resistance. Once rebuilt in 2006, it will become a symbol of reconstruction. One would be without faith if one ignored the opportunity this represents.

Reinelt: Together, we Protestants and Catholics have often experienced a communion of severe suffering in this country. I find it especially rewarding that we are strongly united in the desire to reach out to those who are outside the churches. This is a burning issue for any real Christian. This community between us will bear fruit because Christ acts within it.

Kress: The people among whom we live as Christians do not ask us if we are Protestant or Catholic. They want to know if we are Christians. They want to know how Christianity affects one's life. This question is directed at us jointly. And this assigns us the beautiful task to seek as much community as possible without any of us refuting our traditions.

~~~~~

The Rev. Volker Kress is bishop of the territorial Lutheran Church (*Landeskirche*) of Saxony. The Most Rev. Joachim Reinelt is bishop of the Catholic diocese of Dresden and Meissen in Saxony.

POSTMODERN PENTECOST

CHERYL BRIDGES JOHNS

The world at the dawn of the twenty-first century is a complex array of environmental problems, economic roller coasters, governmental upheavals, terrorism, and viruses such as AIDS that threaten the viability of whole civilizations. Amid this era of chaos there exists a longing for new forms of human community that will provide stability. Yet this dream seems elusive because the values that once provided guidance and identity have given way to a multitude of lifestyle choices and religious beliefs.

Perhaps the biblical prototype of the failed project of Babel best fits our time. Whole "towers of civilization," such as the Soviet Union, have collapsed, dispersing people and reclaiming ancient ethnic identities. Common languages are giving way to regional tongues, and shared visions of reality are being replaced by warring cultural and religious beliefs.

The world that is postmodern is now underway, and nothing can be taken for granted. We have to adjust to life after Babel. How does Christianity not only survive, but thrive, in such a setting? I believe the answer lies in recognizing the defining place of Pentecost in the ongoing life and mission of the church.

Each year the church relives the story of salvation through the celebrations of Advent, Christmas, Lent, Holy Week, Good Friday, Easter, Ascension, and Pentecost. As the last feast of the first part of the church year, Pentecost signals, in one sense, the climax of the Christian story. It is in the coming of the Holy Spirit on Pentecost that the goal of the other feasts is achieved, namely, the pouring out of God's Spirit upon "all flesh," so "everyone who calls on the name of the Lord will be saved" (Acts 2:21).

Pentecost marks the fulfillment of the promise and prayer of Christ for unity among God's people. The Spirit provides a common language that transcends ethnic, racial, social, and economic divisions. In Pentecost the confusion of Babel is reversed. And it is in Pentecost that the life of the church is to be continually renewed through the Spirit's work.

Pentecostalism is a contemporary Christian movement that takes for itself the name of the ancient feast. The movement cannot claim Pentecost as its exclusive right because this feast is a spring of life for the whole church. However, Pentecostalism does contain signs of the significance of Pentecost for "all flesh," the whole of humanity. And it shows Christianity how to survive and thrive in an era characterized by chaos.

Some 500 million people worldwide adhere to Pentecostalism, and their numbers increase daily. This movement arose out of the masses and the dispossessed. It has helped to move the axis of Christianity from the Northern Hemisphere to the Southern. The continents of South America and Africa are replacing Europe and North America as centers of evangelism and mission. The Pentecostal movement has altered the face of Christianity radically throughout the world. The majority of Christians are now nonwhite, female, and live in the major urban centers of the world. In addition, in places such as Africa, Christianity, be it Anglican, Roman Catholic, or evangelical, is primarily Pentecostal in form.

All around the world, where there is great economic and political chaos, Pentecostal Christianity is thriving. In his research on Pentecostalism, Harvard's Harvey Cox has taken note of the movement's capacity to thrive in places characterized by cultural upheaval. He sees this as a result of Pentecostalism's remarkable ability to "lure anarchy into the sacred circle and tame it" (from *Fire from Heaven: The Rise of Pentecostal Spirituality* [Reading, Mass.: Addison-Wesley, 1995]). He notes that the deep struggle of the future is the struggle between order and chaos and points out how Pentecostals incorporate this struggle into their liturgical life.

Pentecostals believe that people whose lives are characterized by abuse, oppression, addictions, and violence find in Pentecostalism a way to bring their chaos to church where it can be named, overcome, and negated. The old paradigm of defining religious movements among the oppressed as escapist and an opiate to numb the pain of daily existence is now giving way to a more adequate description of what actually occurs in the lives of people.

The pathos of life is not ignored. Rather, Pentecostals express this pathos through worship practices such as testimonies, songs, and prayers. Struggles and hardships are expressed, not to be escaped but to be overcome. The pain of life may be strong, but God's transforming power in Christ is stronger. That is why Pentecostals are not afraid to invite chaos to church. They believe the Spirit is there waiting.

In Pentecostal communities—whether in the shantytowns outside the large cities of Africa, the *favelas* of Brazil, or the inner cities of the United States—people find free spaces where they have the opportunity to reinvent themselves. They find that salvation is more comprehensive than what is expressed in the mainstream churches' theological language. Redemption is a package deal that affects all of human existence. It is deliverance from the powers that hold sway over the lives of people. Life itself can be transformed out of chaos into order.

Yet it is a mistake to label Pentecostal religion as a form of fundamentalism. Pentecostalism is first and foremost a religion of the spirit and not the letter of the Law. It is a religion that offers freedom, breaking down long-established barriers that create race, gender, and economic divisions. It is not usually articulated in precise formulations but in concrete action that is often fluid and adaptive to culture. It is a gospel of transformation more than a gospel of right behavior. Fundamentalism attempts to wall out chaos by constructing a fortress out of rigid moral codes. Pentecostalism goes into the territory controlled by darkness and creates a liberation zone.

In addition, Pentecostalism is thriving in the postmodern world because it contains elements of wholesome deconstruction. It dismantles the Enlightenment myth of the human as self-grounded. The spirit of Pentecost, adherents believe, is a fire that burns away any pretense that humans are autonomous individuals guided by reason. And it mocks the spirit of Babel as an illusion of grandeur. It reduces human language (the self's last hiding place) to babble, and in so doing, it reverses the curse of Babel. The language of Pentecost is a new common language that unites God's people under the Word of God.

Only time will tell how Pentecostalism matures and what role it will play in human history, but at present it reminds us that to adequately address the human condition of the twenty-first century, God's people must not be afraid to enter the fray between order and chaos. The Creator Spirit, who brooded over the primordial void, bringing order out of chaos, will transform and renew postmodern men and women and equip them to impact their world for Christ.

~~~~~

The Rev. Dr. Cheryl Bridges Johns is professor of Christian formation and discipleship at the Church of God Theological Seminary, Cleveland, Tennessee.

Epilogue

THE TRINITARIAN REMEDY

UWE SIEMON-NETTO

The images of hijacked airplanes slamming into the World Trade Center in New York and the Pentagon on the outskirts of Washington, D.C. on September 11, 2001, ought to have given postmodern people pause. What kind of faith drove the perpetrators of these crimes? What kind of god were they trying to please? More disquieting, perhaps, is why did they think American society, which is essentially Christian, had this coming? Why did they deem the United States spiritually insolvent and, therefore, worthy only of destruction?

To explore these questions in-depth would go well beyond the scope of this volume. However, one detail of the September 11 drama might give us a hint: the curious case of John Walker Lindh, the American Taliban on whom almost the entire nation has directed its wrath. To be sure, nothing seemed endearing about this well-to-do kid from California who turned on his own people and, when caught, spoke with a faux Arab accent. But upon reflection,

Lindh seemed a paradigm of postmodernity's bankruptcy. If anybody should wonder why some feel only contempt for this egocentric, scatterbrained society in which we live, ask Lindh. What he experienced in Marin County doubtless squares with the distorted image of the United States spanning the globe via the airwaves—the image of a people that lost its way.

It is a caricature, of course, the image of an individualism gone awry, of people tailoring their own god according to their selfish needs. Think of the milieu in which Lindh was raised: There was his father, a Catholic of sorts, but with a faith insufficiently strong to keep him from leaving home for another man. There was his mother, a born-again Buddhist of sorts who also dabbled in American Indian spirituality. There was the "enlightened" neighborhood that found the array of values to which this boy was exposed ever so chic.

Well, John Walker Lindh clearly yearned for something else. Like so many Westerners who are falling for stern, law-centered religions such as Mormonism or Islam, he sought the firm hand of the almighty. Post-Enlightenment ambiguities seemed as unpersuasive to him as they were to postmodern America's detractors in the Muslim world and beyond. As the Lutheran theologian Paul R. Hinlicky wrote, postmodernity's quintessential prophecy was Friedrich Nietzsche's word that a new paganism would put an end to Christendom.

Seen from this perspective, the strict monotheists' scorn for the neopagan Western fun society, in which everybody does his or her "own thing," seems almost understandable. To say this does not justify what Osama bin Laden's men, Walker included, have done. It is simply a sad observation of how the Christian message, which is vastly more exciting than the frightening subservience Muhammad imposes on people in

Islam, has increasingly failed to grab people's imagination since the late seventeenth century.

Jokes have been made about God's acts of love for us whom He created in His own image. "We don't need bleeding men hanging from crosses," declared feminist theologians of assorted "Christian" denominations at "re-imaging" conferences at which, in mock eucharistic meals, female body juices were celebrated with milk and honey. It became fashionable to blaspheme the Holy Spirit by portraying Him as some kind of adulterous fiend—an image as offensive to Muslims as it is to faithful Christians because the Qur'an, too, says that the mother of Christ was a virgin.

To get back to Lindh: One wonders what kind of catechism he was taught in the church he attended as a child with his father. One wonders why this clearly inquisitive boy was not stirred by the magnificence of Christianity's unique story that the Almighty made Himself weak and small and ultimately paid a gruesome price for our wretchedness. One wonders what nonsense Lindh might have been told about the Holy Spirit, that person of the Holy Trinity postmodern people tend to abuse most by wantonly slaughtering the life He has created before it is even born.

Postmodern humans seem to have become incapable of grasping the whole beauty of Christianity's trinitarian faith, in which the free-blowing Spirit proceeds from the Father and the Son chiefly for our benefit. Numbed by media noise, people fail to see that without the Spirit they will recognize nothing of the divine—neither the Father's faithfulness nor the Son's redeeming love, neither God's creation nor the role the Creator has assigned to us as His cooperators in the ongoing process of creation.

Without the Spirit, we fall into the Enlightenment trap of abolishing the whole concept of a divinely created order by transferring the ultimate rank from creation to our curiosity about the universe. Without the Spirit, we lose our sense of reality; the magnificence of God's work is not the essence anymore but whatever glimpses of it our limited minds manage to catch. To give the most recent example, without the Spirit, postmodern people do not marvel at the intricate design of the now deciphered human genome; indeed, it is even considered disreputable in academia to discuss, as Willam Dembski does, intelligent design. All postmodernity allows us to celebrate is the genome's decoding, as if this achievement were not in itself a gift of the Spirit.

By dismissing the Holy Trinity, the postmodern person, whose marks include autism, also misses the divine pattern for his or her own existence. And this is the pattern: As God in His triune nature lives in community, so are we, who are created in His image, meant to live communally—as one flesh in marriage and family, as the one body of Christ in the church, and ultimately, in eternity, with one another and with God. By discarding trinitarian thinking, we dispense with the freedom brought to us by the Spirit and opt for either slavery in chaos or slavery to a haughty deity.

It is, therefore, high time for theologians to begin looking for trinitarian answers to postmodernity's catastrophic disarray—or its harsh alternative: John Walker Lindh's and Osama bin Laden's version of Islam. Ever-changing forms of "spirituality" will not get us out of this Nietzschean dilemma; ever-new discoveries about the universe won't do it either, unless they are informed by the Holy Spirit.

Postmodernity is the final and most absurd stage of our quest for autonomy. This path was first trod in the French Revolution, as Dietrich Bonhoeffer reminds us. It ended in nihilism. "The liberation of man as an absolute ideal leads only to man's self-destruction," wrote Bonhoeffer, who was hanged precisely because he had understood the mortal peril of this and acted upon it.

If the pursuit of autonomy is lethal and, therefore, wrong, what are we to seek? Freedom! Paul tells us—and

Martin Luther never ceases to remind us—that God wants us to be free and that Christ is the path to freedom. This is why from their different perspectives all the authors in this volume have pointed to Christ as the remedy for postmodernity's woes.

But Paul also makes it clear that there is no way to grasp Christ except through the Spirit's counsel. Hence, postmodernity's profusion of bogus and ever-changing "truths" and "values" can only be overcome by a renewal of trinitarian theology—not in the watered-down version of liberal theology: No cheap anthropocentric metaphors are in order here. Rather, theologians must learn to speak about the triune God in a new language that resonates with post-postmodern people who are attempting to come out of the spiritual bankruptcy into which the quest for autonomy has led them. This may well be one of the most important tasks for theologians in the almost 2,000 years of church history. It is an urgent task. There is no time to lose.

FOR FURTHER READING

Allen, Diogenes. *Postmodern Theology: Christian Faith in a Pluralist World*. San Francisco: Harper & Row, 1989.

Anderson, Walter Truett. *Reality Isn't What It Used to Be*. San Francisco: Harper & Row, 1992.

Brown, Frank Burch. *Good Taste, Bad Taste, and Christian Taste*. Oxford, 2000.

Domanska, Ewa, ed. *Encounters: Philosophy of History after Postmodernism*. University of Virginia Press, 1998. (Contains interviews with historians known for their postmodernist views, but the few moral traditionalists in the book have the strongest interviews.)

Dyrness, William A. *Visual Faith: Art, Theology, and Worship in Dialogue*. Grand Rapids: Baker, 2001.

Grenz, Stanley. *A Primer on Postmodernism*. Grand Rapids: Eerdmans, 1996.

Griffin, David Ray. *God and Religion in the Postmodern World: Essays in Postmodern Theology*. Albany: SUNY Press, 1989.

Harvey, David. *The Condition of Postmodernity: An Enquiry into the Origins of Cultural Change*. Oxford: Basil Blackwell, 1989.

Heelas, Paul, with David Martin and Paul Morris. *Religion, Modernity, and Postmodernity*. Oxford: Basil Blackwell, 1998.

Hinlicky, Paul R. "The Spirit of Christ Amid the Spirits of the Post-Modern World." *Lutheran Quarterly* 4 (2000).

Junker-Kenny, Maureen, et al. *Faith in a Society of Instant Gratification*. Maryknoll: Orbis, 1999.

Kroker. Arthur. *The Possessed Individual: Technology and the French Postmodern*. New York: St. Martin's, 1992.

————. *Varieties of Postmodern Theology.* Albany: SUNY Press, 1989.

Lakeland, Paul. *Postmodernity: Christian Identity in a Fragmented Age.* Minneapolis: Fortress, 1997.

Lyotard, Jean-Francois. *The PostModern Condition.* Minneapolis: University of Minnesota Press, 1978.

————. *Toward the PostModern.* Atlantic Highlands: Humanities Press, 1993.

Marion, Jean-Luc. *God without Being.* Chicago: University of Chicago Press, 1991.

McClure, John S. *Other-Wise Preaching: A Postmodern Ethic for Homiletics.* St. Louis: Chalice, 2001.

Middleton, J. Richard. *Truth Is Stranger Than It Used to Be: Biblical Faith in a Postmodern Age.* Downers Grove: InterVarsity, 1995.

Milbank, John. *Theology and the Social Theory: Beyond Secular Reason.* Oxford: Blackwell, 1990.

Pattison, George. *Art, Modernity, and Faith.* SCM Press, 1991, 1998.

Spitzer, Alan B. *Historical Truth and Lies about the Past: Reflections on Dewey, Dreyfus, de Man, and Reagan.* University of North Carolina Press, 1996. (A clear account of how all sorts of people trust in notions of truth when their backs are pressed to the wall.)

Veith, Gene Edward. *Postmodern Times: A Christian Guide to Contemporary Thought and Culture.* Wheaton: Crossway, 1994.

————. *State of the Arts.* Wheaton: Crossway, 2001.

Viladesau, Richard. *Theology and the Arts.* Paulist Press, 2000.

von Huyssteen, Wentzel. *Duet or Duel? Theology and Science in a Postmodern World.* Harrisburg: Trinity Press Internaitonal, 1998.

Ward, Glenn. *Teach Yourself Postmodernism.* London: Hodder & Stoughton, 1997.

Ward, Graham. *The Postmodern God: A Theological Reader.* Oxford: Basil Blackwell, 1997.

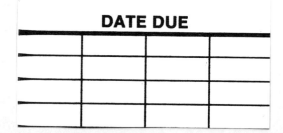